Bradley's

GIANT

15th Updated Edition

PIANO BOOK

Pop • Movies • TV • Classics • Patriotic • Standards

Arranged by Richard Bradley

© MMVII BRADLEY PUBLICATIONS
All Rights Assigned to and Controlled by ALFRED PUBLISHING CO., INC.

ISBN-10: 0-7390-4551-2
ISBN-13: 978-0-7390-4551-0

Alfred

ALPHABETICAL CONTENTS

24 (END TITLE THEME) 212

ALSO SPRACH ZARATHUSTRA 154

AMERICA (MY COUNTRY 'TIS OF THEE) 260

AMERICA, THE BEAUTIFUL 231

ANCHORS AWEIGH 234

AS TIME GOES BY 114

AT LAST 275

BALLAD OF GILLIGAN'S ISLE, THE 228

BATTLE HYMN OF THE REPUBLIC, THE 255

BECAUSE YOU LOVED ME 102

BEFORE YOUR LOVE 6

BIG YELLOW TAXI 82

BLUE MOON 291

BOSS OF ME (THEME FROM "MALCOLM IN THE MIDDLE") 201

BREAKAWAY 86

CAISSONS GO ROLLING ALONG, THE 239

CALIFORNIA 194

CAN'T FIGHT THE MOONLIGHT 66

CANON IN D 174

CLAIR DE LUNE (FIRST THEME) 162

EBB TIDE 281

EMBRACEABLE YOU 296

ER (MAIN THEME) 210

EVERYBODY LOVES RAYMOND (MAIN TITLE) 206

FAR AWAY 44

FLIGHT OF THE BUMBLE-BEE, THE 180

FUNERAL MARCH OF THE MARIONETTES 184

FÜR ELISE (MAIN THEME) 160

GAME OF LOVE, THE 20

GOOD OL' BOYS 222

HEART 265

HERO 72

HOME 12

HOW DO I LIVE 146

HOW DO YOU KEEP THE MUSIC PLAYING? 143

HUNGARIAN RHAPSODY NO. 2 178

I DON'T WANT TO MISS A THING 106

I GOT A NAME 138

I'LL BE THERE FOR YOU 216

IT'S DE-LOVELY 284

KING OF THE HILL 208

LIKE WE NEVER LOVED AT ALL 27

LULLABY 170

MARCH OF THE PENGUINS (THE HARSHEST PLACE ON EARTH) 127

MARINE'S HYMN, THE (FROM THE HALLS OF MONTEZUMA) 242

MISTY. 301

MOONLIGHT SONATA (OP. 27, NO. 2) 164

MY FUNNY VALENTINE 272

NOTEBOOK, THE (MAIN TITLE). 99

NORWEIGAN DANCE. 172

OVER THE RAINBOW 118

PINK PANTHER, THE 124

PLATOON SWIMS 96

ROSE, THE. 111

SAVE THE LAST DANCE FOR ME 39

SECOND TIME AROUND, THE. 294

SHAPE OF MY HEART 62

SINGIN' IN THE RAIN 121

SMOOTH. 78

SOAK UP THE SUN. 50

SOMEONE TO WATCH OVER ME. 278

SONG FROM M*A*S*H. 189

SORCERER'S APPRENTICE, THE 151

STAR WARS® (MAIN TITLE). 136

STAR-SPANGLED BANNER, THE. 262

STARS AND STRIPES FOREVER, THE 248

THEME FROM "THE ANDY GRIFFITH SHOW" 226

THEME FROM ICE CASTLES (THROUGH THE EYES OF LOVE) 92

THEME FROM "NYPD BLUE" 214

THEME FROM SWAN LAKE. 186

THIS I PROMISE YOU 56

U. S. AIR FORCE, THE (THE WILD BLUE YONDER) 236

UN BEL DÌ 168

WEST WING, THE (MAIN TITLE) 192

WHAT A WONDERFUL WORLD 288

WHEN I FALL IN LOVE 268

WHEN JOHNNY COMES MARCHING HOME. 252

WHEN THE STARS GO BLUE. 34

WHERE OR WHEN. 298

WILLIAM TELL OVERTURE 156

WONKA'S WELCOME SONG 132

YANKEE DOODLE. 258

YOU'RE A GRAND OLD FLAG 245

CONTENTS BY CATEGORY

POP

BEFORE YOUR LOVE . . . . KELLY CLARKSON 6
BIG YELLOW TAXI . . . . COUNTING CROWS FEATURING VANESSA CARLTON . . . 82
BREAKAWAY . . . . KELLY CLARKSON 86
CAN'T FIGHT THE MOONLIGHT . . . . LEANN RIMES 66
FAR AWAY . . . . NICKELBACK 44
GAME OF LOVE, THE . . . . SANTANA FEATURING MICHELLE BRANCH 20
HERO . . . . ENRIQUE IGLESIAS 72
HOME . . . . MICHAEL BUBLÉ 12
LIKE WE NEVER LOVED AT ALL . . . . FAITH HILL 27
SAVE THE LAST DANCE FOR ME . . . . MICHAEL BUBLÉ 39
SHAPE OF MY HEART . . . . BACKSTREET BOYS 62
SMOOTH . . . . SANTANA FEATURING ROB THOMAS 121
SOAK UP THE SUN . . . . SHERYL CROW 50
THIS I PROMISE YOU . . . . *NSYNC 56
WHEN THE STARS GO BLUE . . . . TIM MCGRAW 34

MOVIES

AS TIME GOES BY . . . . CASABLANCA 114
BECAUSE YOU LOVED ME . . . . UP CLOSE & PERSONAL 102
HOW DO I LIVE . . . . CON AIR 146
HOW DO YOU KEEP THE MUSIC PLAYING? . . . . BEST FRIENDS 143
I DON'T WANT TO MISS A THING . . . . ARMAGEDDON 106
I GOT A NAME . . . . INVINCIBLE 138
MARCH OF THE PENGUINS
    (THE HARSHEST PLACE ON EARTH) . . . . MARCH OF THE PENGUINS 127
NOTEBOOK, THE (MAIN TITLE) . . . . THE NOTEBOOK 99
OVER THE RAINBOW . . . . THE WIZARD OF OZ 118
PINK PANTHER, THE . . . . THE PINK PANTHER 124
PLATOON SWIMS . . . . FLAGS OF OUR FATHERS 96
ROSE, THE . . . . THE ROSE 111
SINGIN' IN THE RAIN . . . . SINGIN' IN THE RAIN 121
STAR WARS (MAIN TITLE) . . . . STAR WARS 136
THEME FROM ICE CASTLES
    (THROUGH THE EYES OF LOVE) . . . . ICE CASTLES 92
WONKA'S WELCOME SONG . . . . CHARLIE AND THE CHOCOLATE FACTORY 132

TV

24 (END TITLE THEME) 24 212
BALLAD OF GILLIGAN'S ISLE, THE . . . . GILLIGAN'S ISLAND 228
BOSS OF ME
    (THEME FROM "MALCOLM IN THE MIDDLE") . . . . MALCOLM IN THE MIDDLE 201
CALIFORNIA . . . . THE O. C. 194
ER (MAIN THEME) . . . . ER 210
EVERYBODY LOVES RAYMOND (MAIN TITLE) . . . . EVERYBODY LOVES RAYMOND 206
GOOD OL' BOYS . . . . THE DUKES OF HAZZARD 222
I'LL BE THERE FOR YOU . . . . FRIENDS 216
KING OF THE HILL . . . . KING OF THE HILL 208
SONG FROM M*A*S*H . . . . M*A*S*H 189
THEME FROM "NYPD BLUE" . . . . NYPD BLUE 214
THEME FROM "THE ANDY GRIFFITH SHOW" . . . . THE ANDY GRIFFITH SHOW 226
WEST WING, THE (MAIN TITLE) . . . . THE WEST WING 192

CLASSICS

ALSO SPRACH ZARATHUSTRA	RICHARD STRAUSS	154
CANON IN D	JOHANN PACHELBEL	174
CLAIR DE LUNE (FIRST THEME)	CLAUDE DEBUSSY	162
FLIGHT OF THE BUMBLE-BEE, THE	NIKOLAY RIMSKY-KORSAKOV	180
FUNERAL MARCH OF THE MARIONETTES	CHARLES GOUNOD	184
FÜR ELISE (MAIN THEME)	LUDWIG VAN BEETHOVEN	160
HUNGARIAN RHAPSODY NO. 2	FRANZ LISZT	178
LULLABY	JOHANNES BRAHMS	170
MOONLIGHT SONATA (OP. 27, NO. 2)	LUDWIG VAN BEETHOVEN	164
NORWEIGAN DANCE	EDVARD GRIEG	172
SORCERER'S APPRENTICE, THE	PAUL DUKAS	151
THEME FROM SWAN LAKE	PETER ILYICH TCHAIKOVSKY	186
UN BEL DÌ	GIACOMO PUCCINI	168
WILLIAM TELL OVERTURE	GIOACCHINO ROSSINI	156

PATRIOTIC

AMERICA (MY COUNTRY 'TIS OF THEE)	260
AMERICA, THE BEAUTIFUL	231
ANCHORS AWEIGH	234
BATTLE HYMN OF THE REPUBLIC, THE	255
CAISSONS GO ROLLING ALONG, THE	239
MARINE'S HYMN, THE (FROM THE HALLS OF MONTEZUMA)	242
STAR-SPANGLED BANNER, THE	262
STARS AND STRIPES FOREVER, THE	248
U.S. AIR FORCE, THE (THE WILD BLUE YONDER)	236
WHEN JOHNNY COMES MARCHING HOME	252
YANKEE DOODLE	258
YOU'RE A GRAND OLD FLAG	245

STANDARDS

AT LAST	275
BLUE MOON	291
EBB TIDE	281
EMBRACEABLE YOU	296
HEART	265
IT'S DE-LOVELY	284
MISTY	301
MY FUNNY VALENTINE	272
SECOND TIME AROUND, THE	294
SOMEONE TO WATCH OVER ME	278
WHAT A WONDERFUL WORLD	288
WHEN I FALL IN LOVE	268
WHERE OR WHEN	298

BEFORE YOUR LOVE

Recorded by Kelly Clarkson

Words and Music by
DESMOND CHILD, GARY BURR
and CATHY DENNIS
Arranged by Richard Bradley

When you go in cir - cles, all the scen - 'ry looks—— the

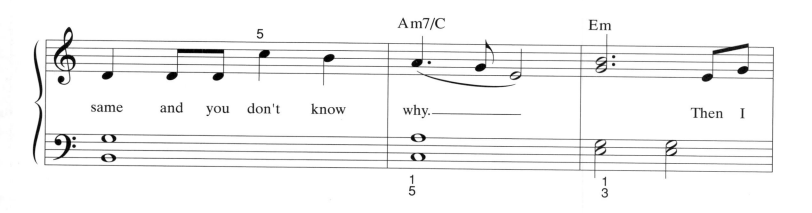

same and you don't know why.———— Then I

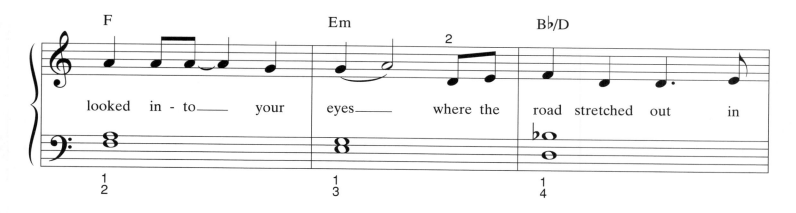

looked in - to—— your eyes—— where the road stretched out in

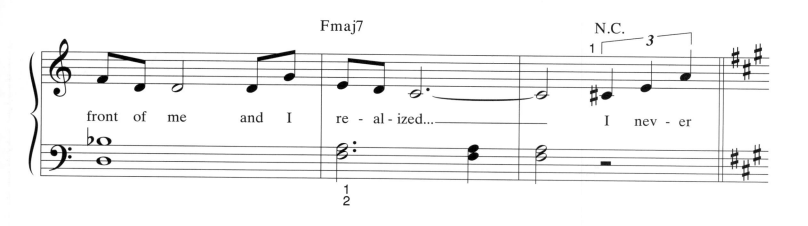

front of me and I re - al - ized...———— I nev - er

8

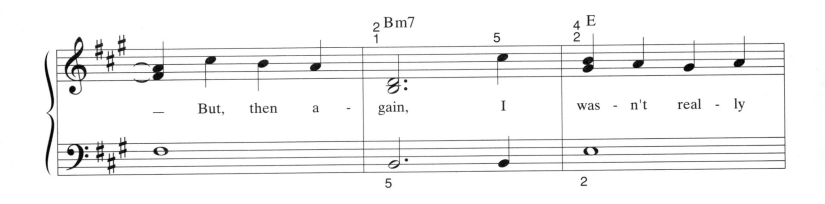

To Coda ⊕

C#m7   F#m7   Bm7

liv - ing.   I nev - er   lived_____ be-

1.
Esus4   E   D2   A/C#

fore_____ your love.

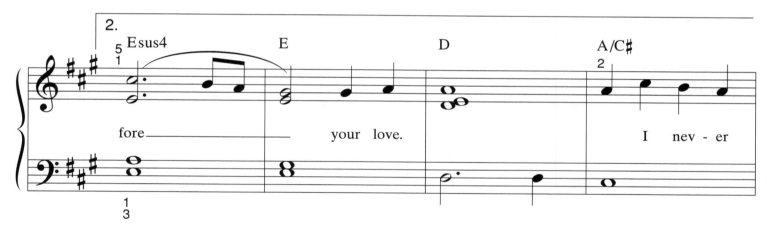

2.
Esus4   E   D   A/C#

fore_____ your love.   I nev - er

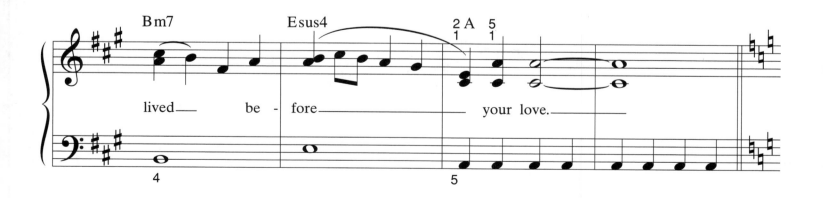

Bm7   Esus4   A

lived___ be - fore_____ your love._____

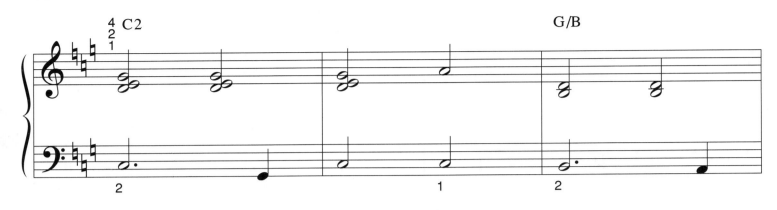

And I don't know why, why the

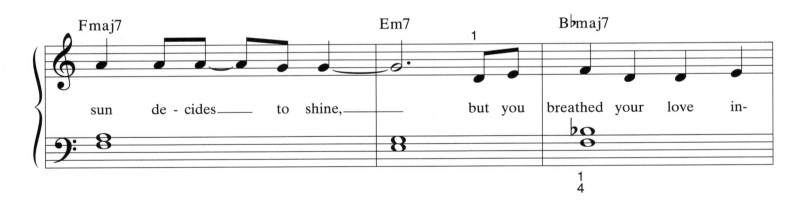

sun de-cides to shine, but you breathed your love in-

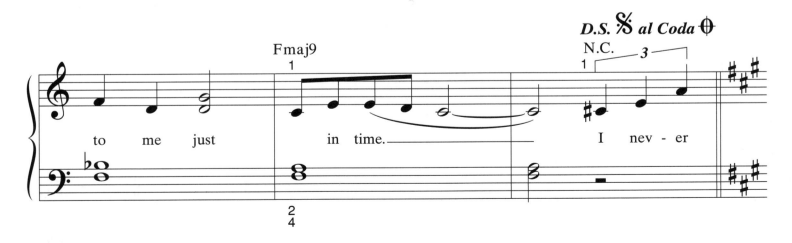

to me just in time. I nev-er

Coda

Verse 2:
I wanted more than just an ordinary life.
All of my dreams seemed like castles in the sky.
I stand before you and my heart is in your hands
And I don't know how I survived without your kiss.
'Cause you've given me a reason to exist.
(To Chorus:)

HOME

Recorded by Michael Bublé

Words and Music by
AMY FOSTER-GILLIES, MICHAEL BUBLÉ
and ALAN CHANG
Arranged by Richard Bradley

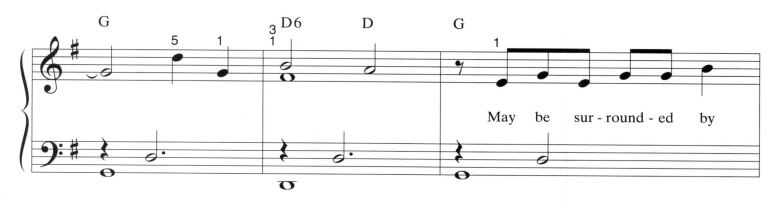

May be sur - round - ed by

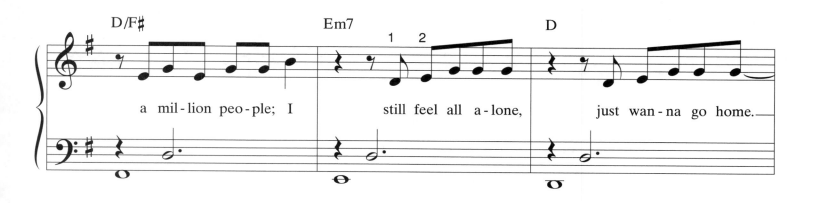

a mil - lion peo - ple; I still feel all a - lone, just wan - na go home.

Oh, I miss you, you know.

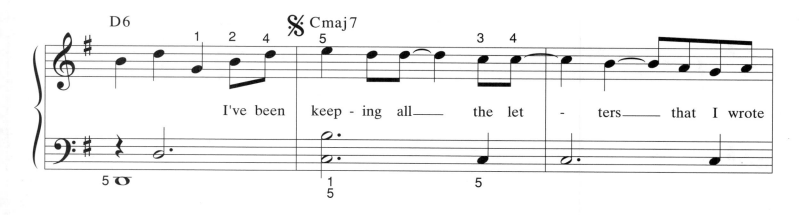

I've been keep - ing all___ the let - ters___ that I wrote

to you,_____ each one a line____ or two,____

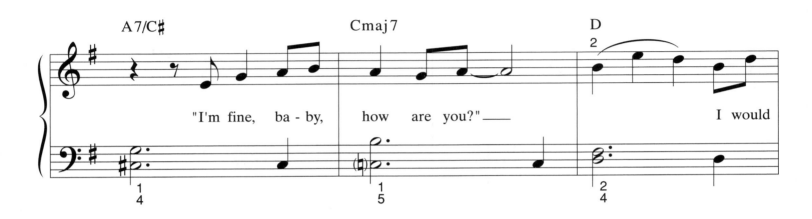

"I'm fine, ba - by, how are you?"____ I would

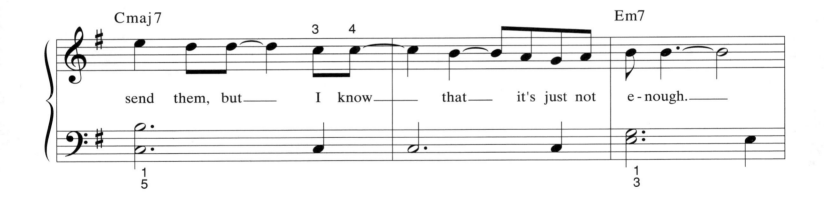

send them, but____ I know____ that____ it's just not e - nough.____

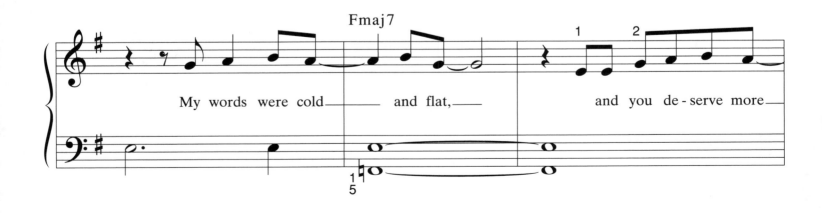

My words were cold____ and flat,____ and you de - serve more____

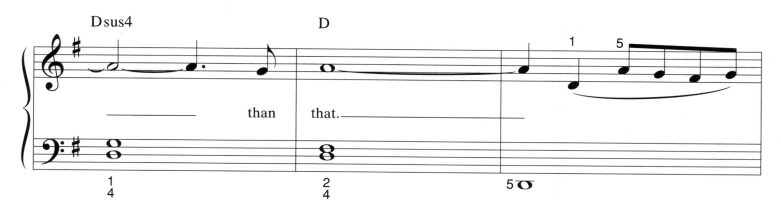

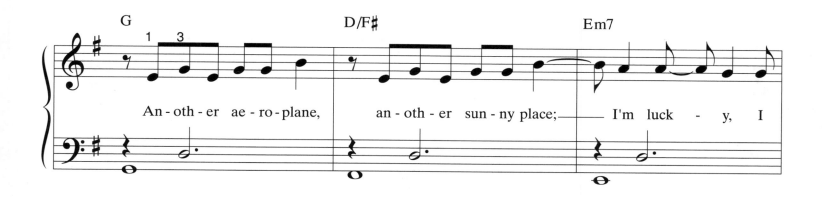

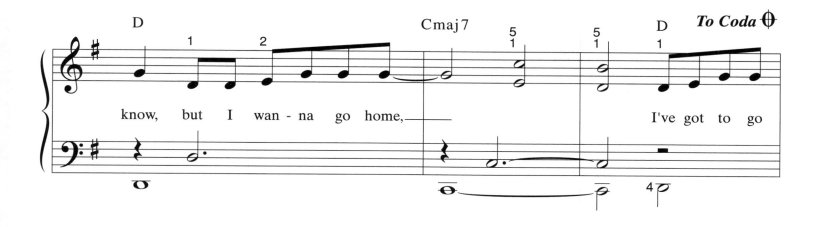

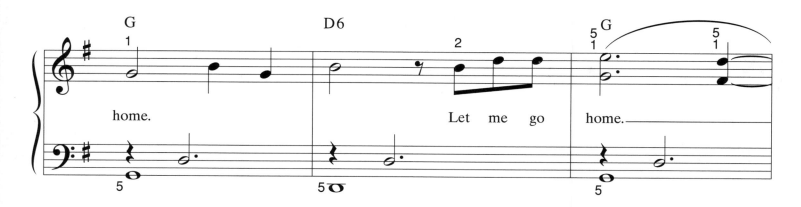

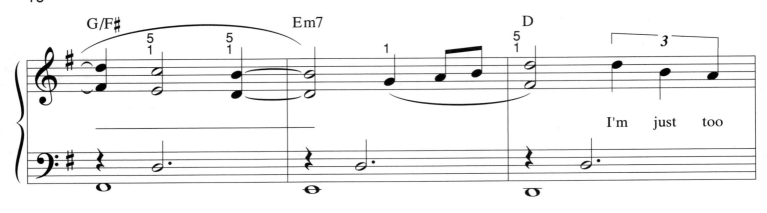

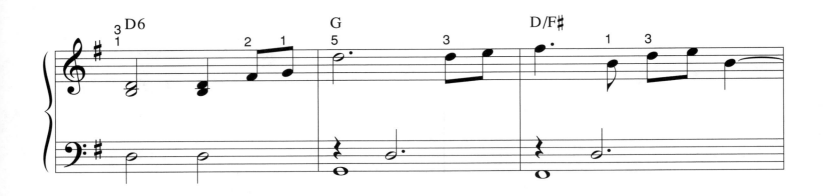

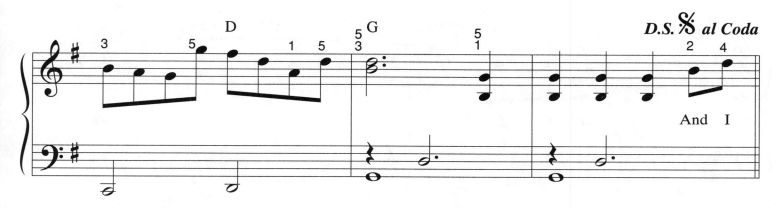

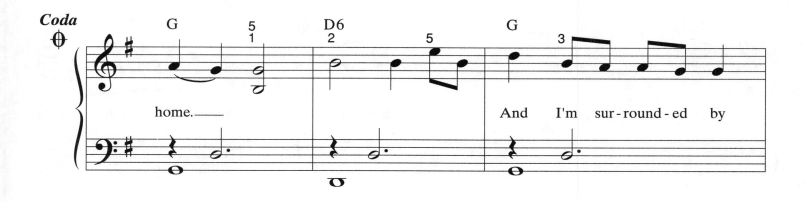

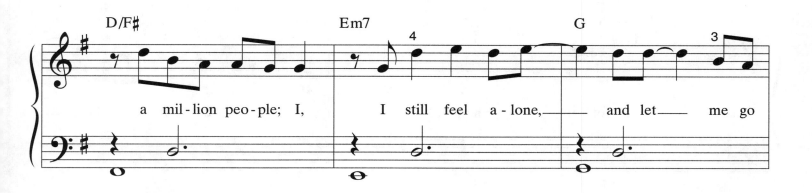

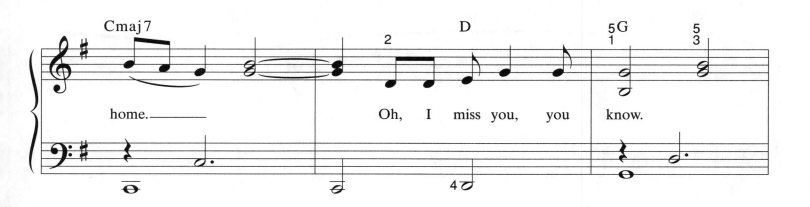

Let me go home.

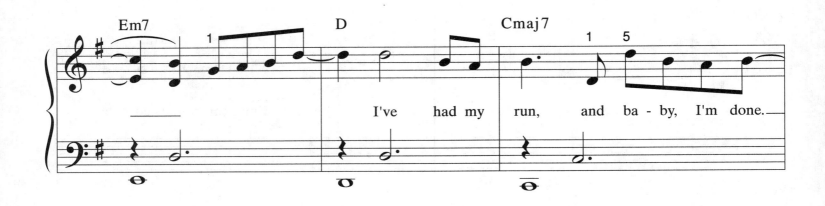

I've had my run, and ba-by, I'm done.

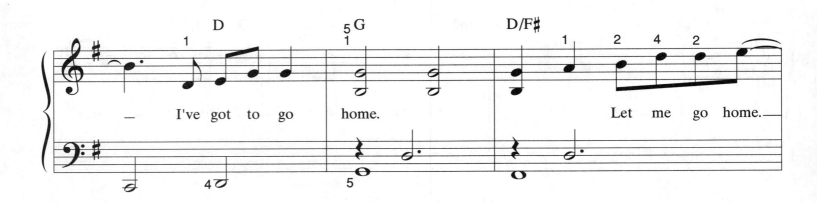

I've got to go home. Let me go home.

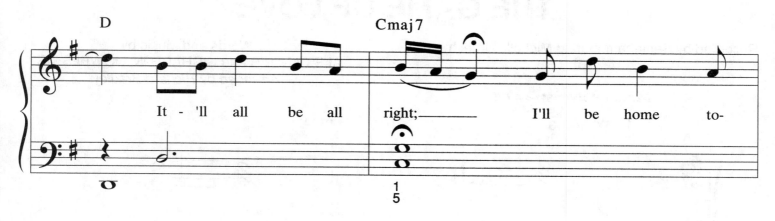

It - 'll all be all right;_____ I'll be home to-

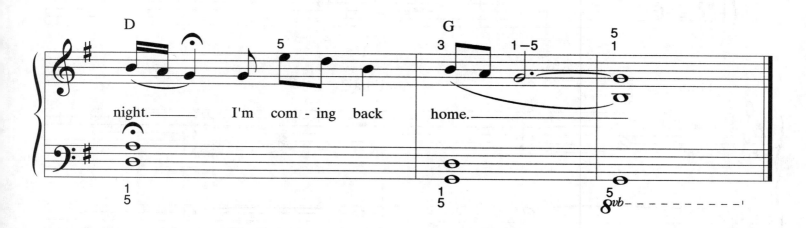

night._____ I'm com - ing back home._____

Verse 2:
And I feel just like I'm living someone else's life.
It's like I just stepped outside when everything was going right.
And I know just why you could not come along with me:
This was not your dream, but you always believed in me.
Another winter day has come and gone away
In either Paris or Rome, and I wanna go home, let me home.

THE GAME OF LOVE

Recorded by Santana featuring Michelle Branch

Words and Music by
ALEX ANDER and RICHARD W. NOWELS, JR.
Arranged by Richard Bradley

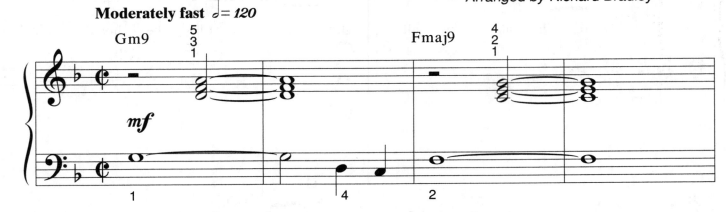

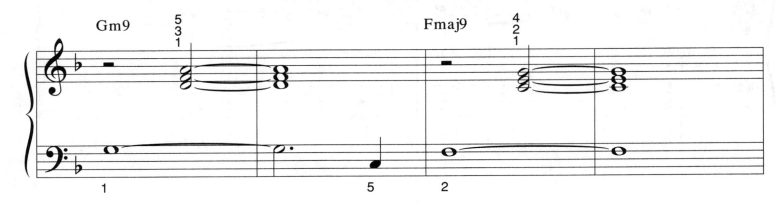

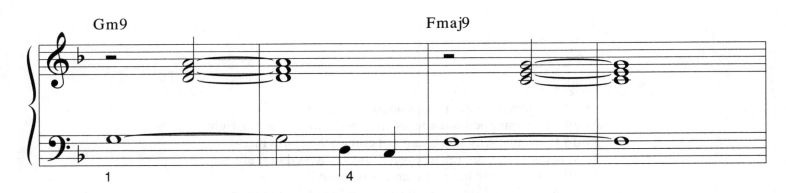

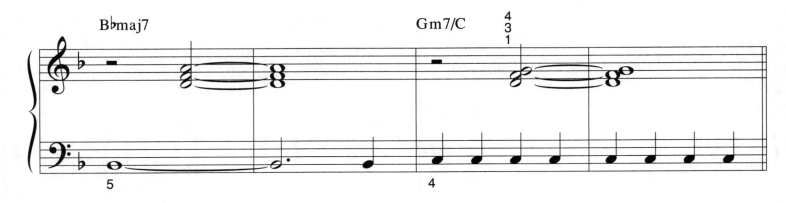

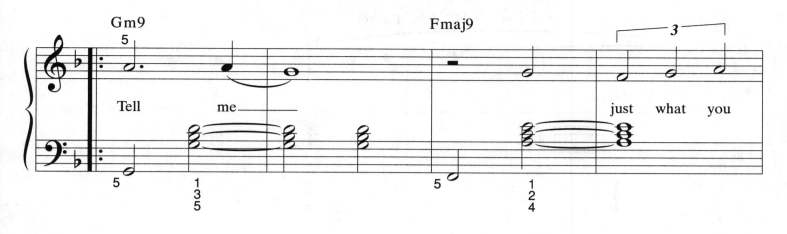

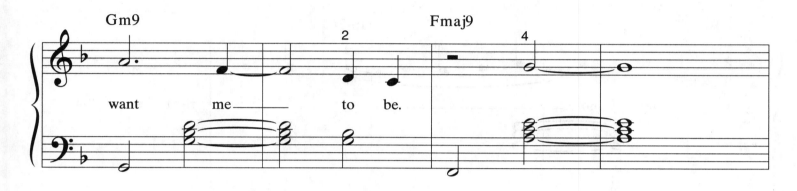

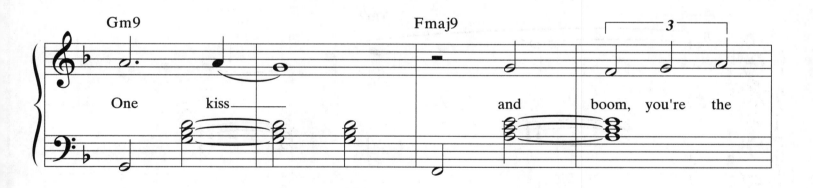

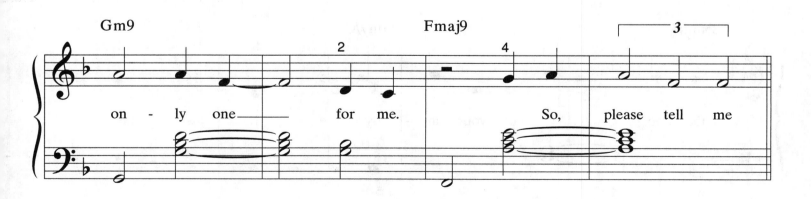

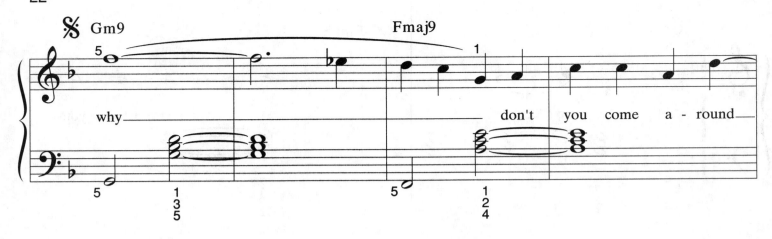

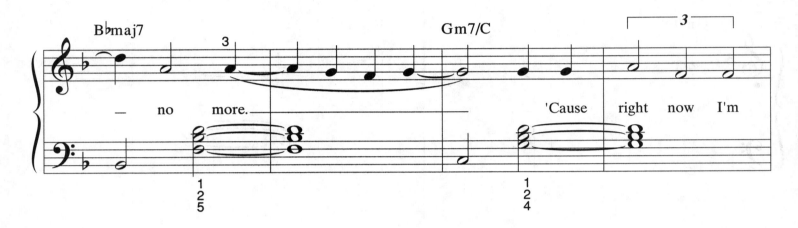

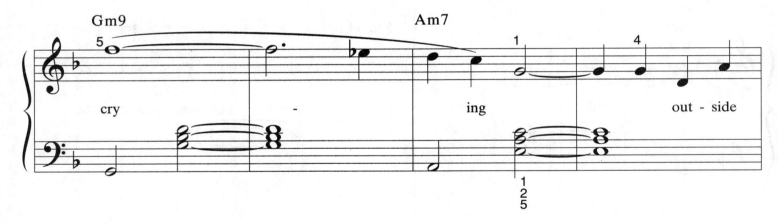

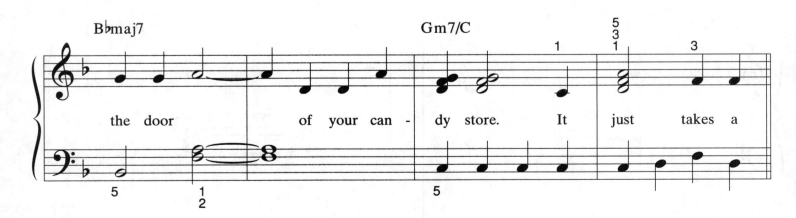

Chorus:

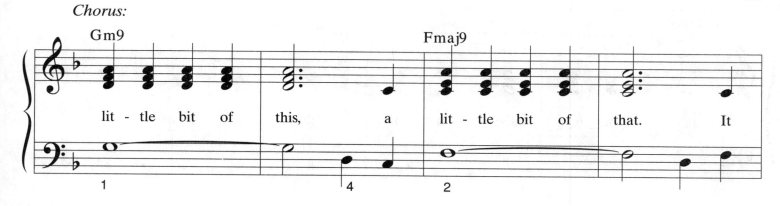

lit - tle bit of this, a lit - tle bit of that. It

start - ed with a kiss, now we're up to bat. A

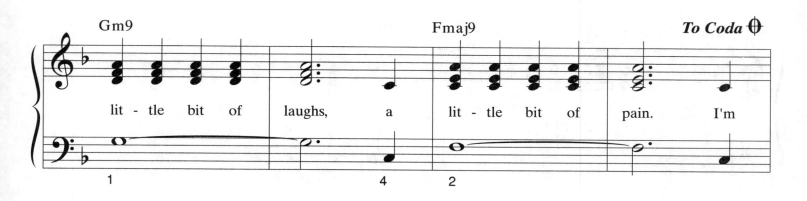

lit - tle bit of laughs, a lit - tle bit of pain. I'm

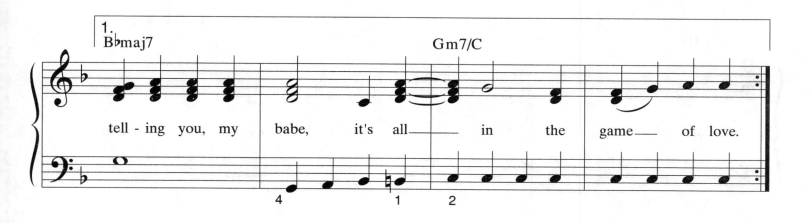

tell - ing you, my babe, it's all in the game of love.

tell - ing you, my babe, it's all in the game of love.

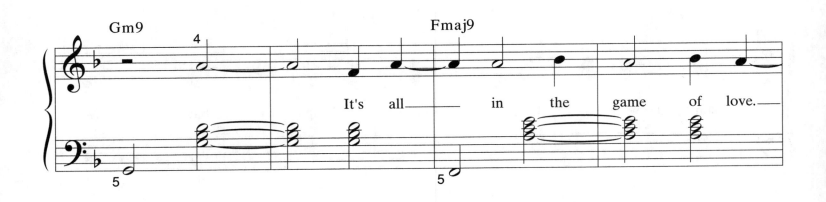

It's all in the game of love.

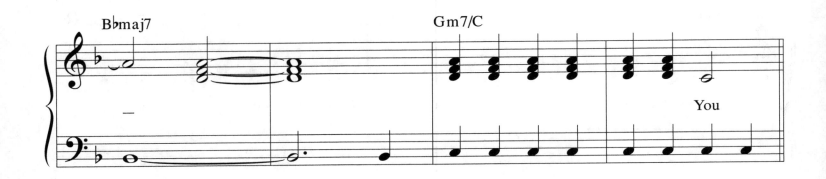

You

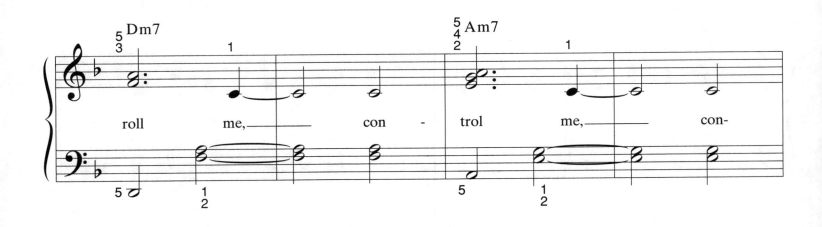

roll me, con - trol me, con-

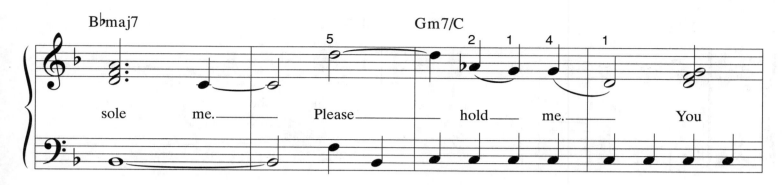

Verse 2:
This, whatever you make it to be,
Sunshine set on the cold, lonely sea.
So please, baby,
Try and use me for what I'm good for.
It ain't saying goodbye,
It's knocking down the door
Of your candy store.
It just takes a . . .
(To Chorus:)

Verse 3:
So, please tell me
Why don't you come around no more.
'Cause right now I'm dying
Outside the door of your loving store
It just takes a . . .
(To Chorus:)

LIKE WE NEVER LOVED AT ALL

Recorded by Faith Hill

Words and Music by
JOHN RICH, VICKY McGEHEE
and SCOTT SACKS
Arranged by Richard Bradley

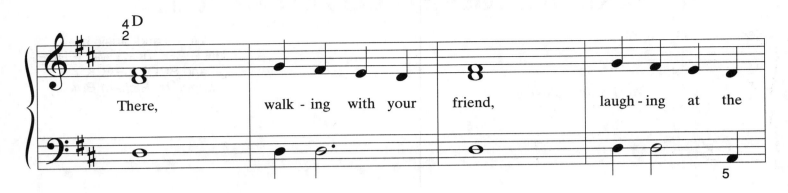

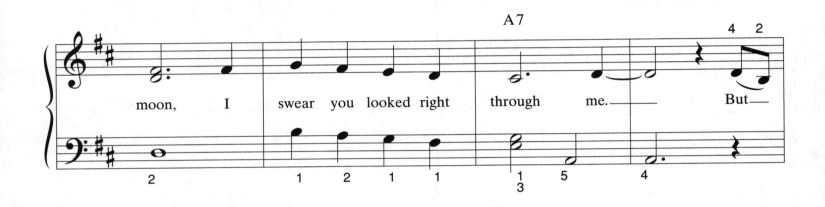

Chorus 1 & 2:

you just walk on by____ with - out one tear in your__ eye?__

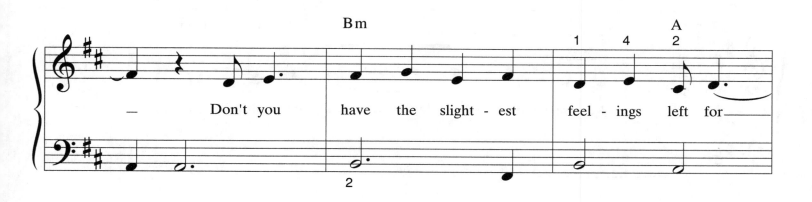

— Don't you have the slight - est feel - ings left for__

— me? May - be that's just your way____ of

deal - ing with the pain,____ for - get - ting ev - 'ry - thing__ be-

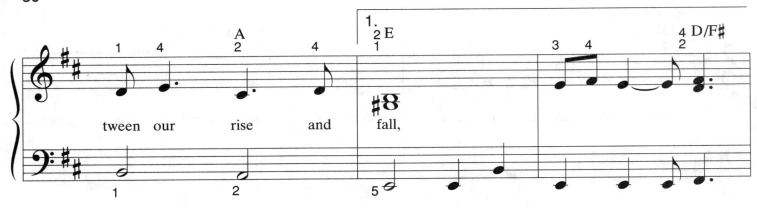

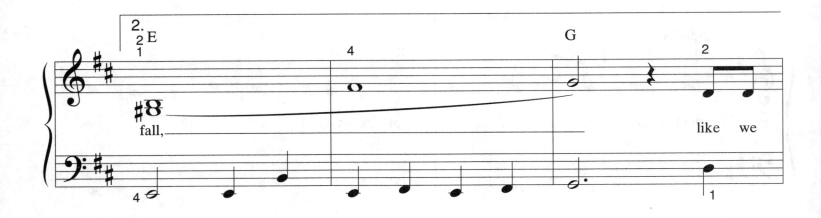

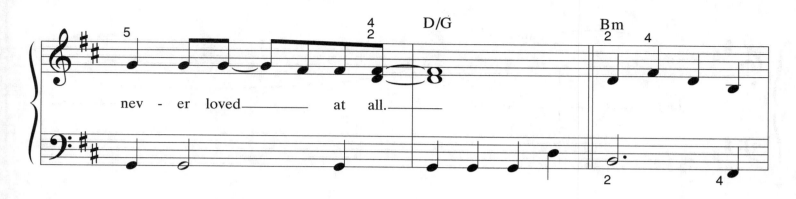

nev - er loved___ at all.___

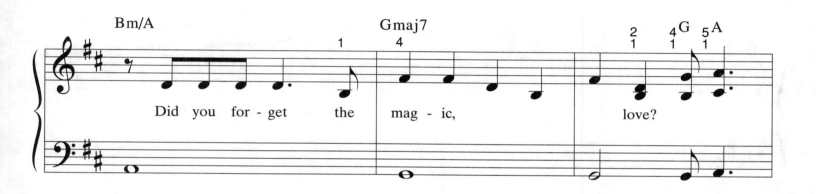

Did you for-get the mag - ic, love?

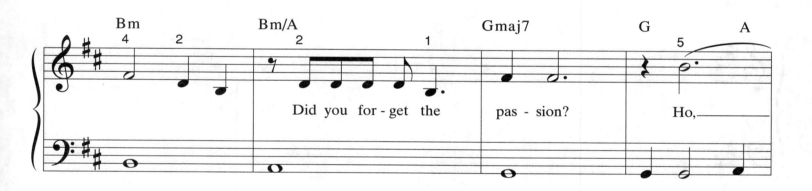

Did you for-get the pas - sion? Ho,___

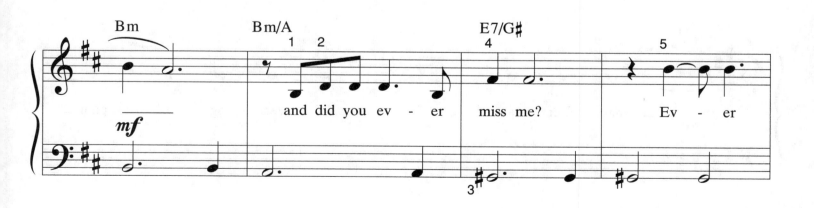

and did you ev - er miss me? Ev - er

Chorus 3:

long _____ to kiss ____ me?

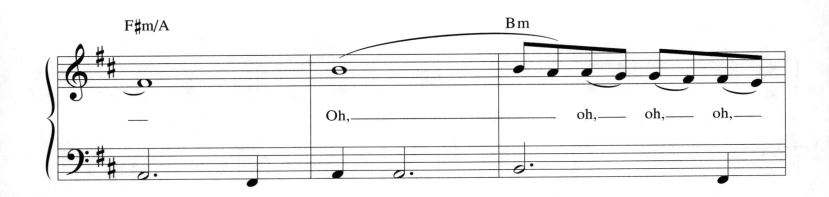

___ Oh, _____ oh, ___ oh, ___ oh, ___

oh, ___ oh, _____ ba - by, _____ ba - by, _____

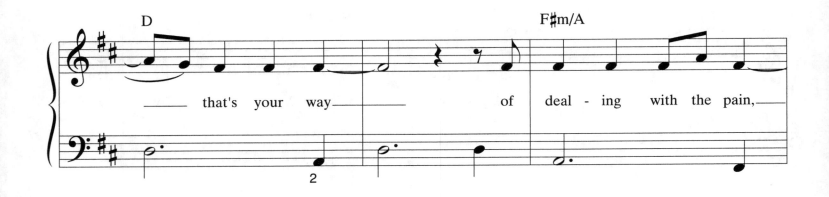

_____ that's your way _____ of deal - ing with the pain,

Verse 2:
You, I hear you're doing fine.
Seems like you're doing well
As far as I can tell.
Time is leaving us behind.
Another week has passed
And still I haven't laughed yet.
So tell me what your secret is
To letting go, letting go like you did,
Like you did. How can . . .
(To Chorus:)

WHEN THE STARS GO BLUE

Recorded by Tim McGraw

Words and Music by
RYAN ADAMS
Arranged by Richard Bradley

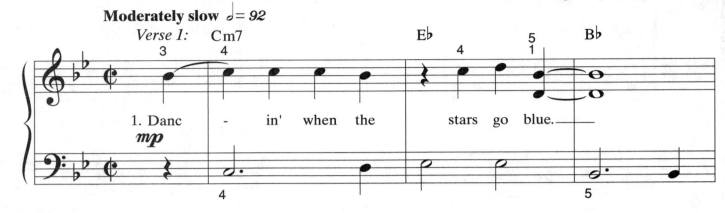

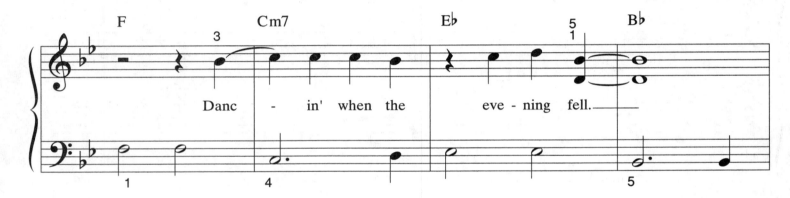

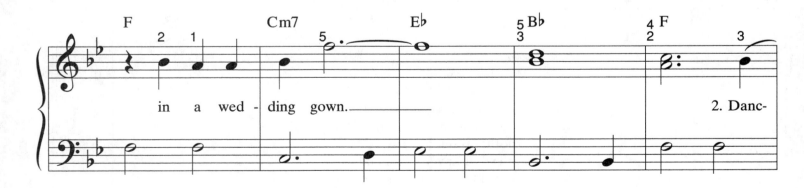

When the Stars Go Blue - 1 - 5

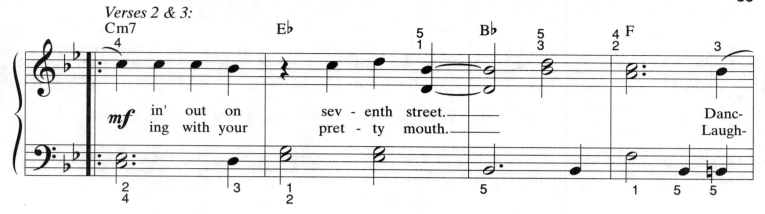

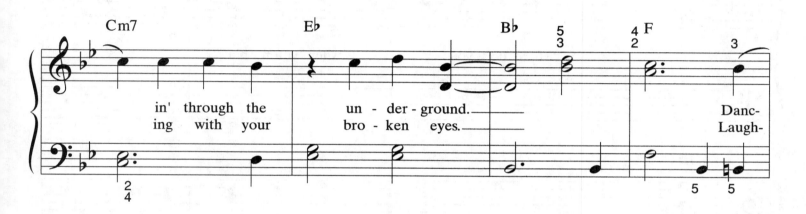

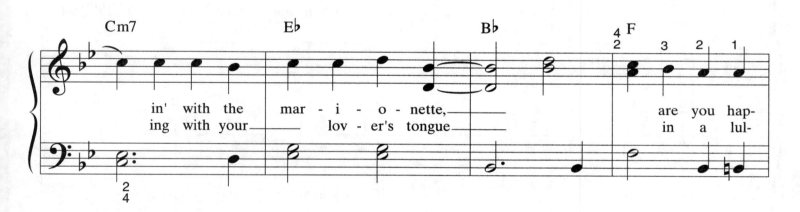

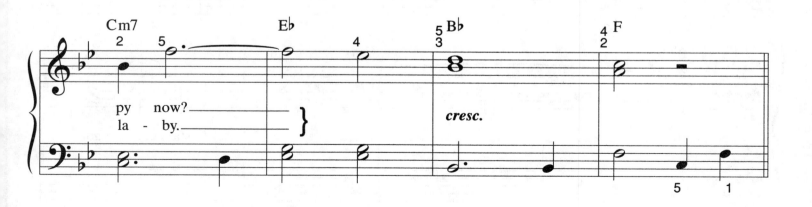

Chorus:

Where do you go ___ when you're lone - ly? ___

Where do you go ___ when you're blue? ___

Where do you go ___ when you're lone - ly? I'll fol-

low you when the stars ___ go

blue, ___ stars ___ go

SAVE THE LAST DANCE FOR ME

Recorded by Michael Bublé

Words and Music by
DOC POMUS and MORT SHUMAN
Arranged by Richard Bradley

You can dance ev - 'ry

know that the

dance with the guy who gave you the eye; let him hold you tight.

mu - sic is fine, like spark - ling wine; go and have your fun.

Save the Last Dance for Me - 1 - 5

You can smile ev - 'ry smile for the man who
Laugh and sing, but while we're a - part____ don't

held your hand____ 'neath the pale moon - light.____ But don't for-
give your heart____ to____ an - y - one.____

get who's tak - ing you home and in whose arms you're

gon - na be.____ So dar - lin',____ save the

1. F

last dance for me.

Oh, I

2. F

N.C.

C7

me.

Ba - by, don't you know I love you so?

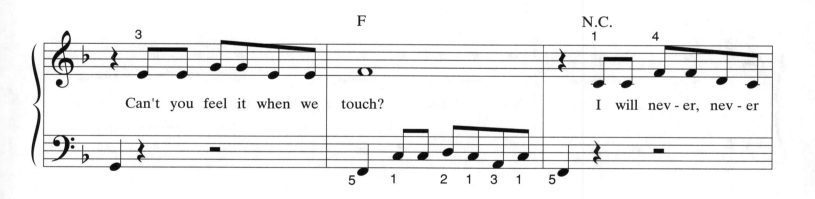

F

N.C.

Can't you feel it when we touch?

I will nev - er, nev - er

C7

F

let you go.

I love you, oh, so much.

Save the Last Dance for Me - 3 - 5

home and in whose arms you're gon - na be.

So, dar - lin', save the last dance for

me. So, dar - lin', save the

last dance for me.

FAR AWAY

Recorded by Nickelback

Lyrics by CHAD KROEGER
Music by NICKELBACK
Arranged by Richard Bradley

Moderately slow ♩= 64

Verse:

This time,— this place,—

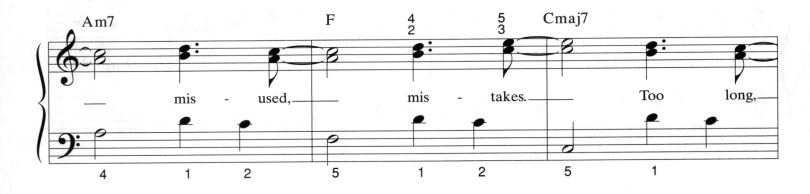

— mis - used,— mis - takes.— Too long,—

— too late.— Who was I— to make— you— wait?

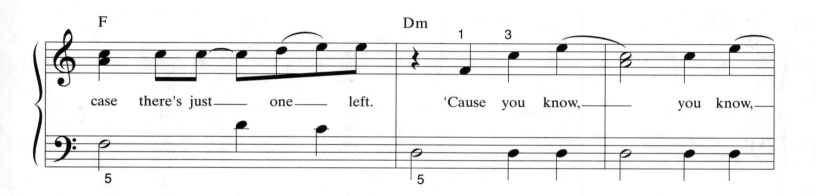

Chorus:

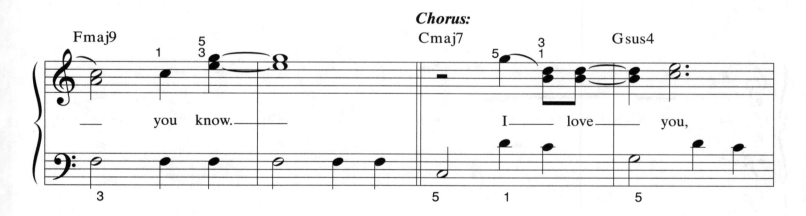

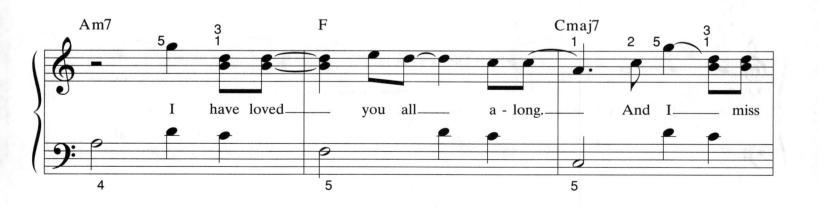

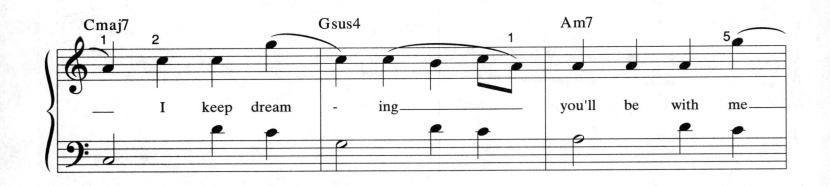

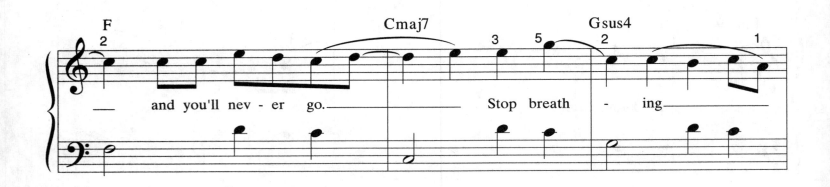

Chorus:

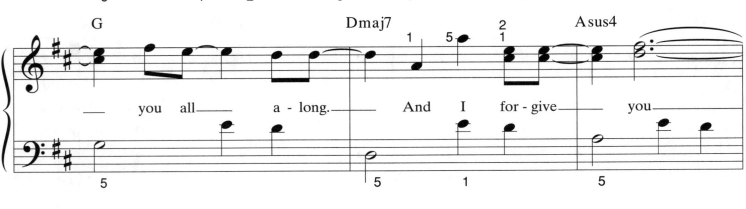

Verse 2:
On my knees, I'll ask last chance for one last dance.
'Cause with you I'd withstand all of hell to hold your hand.
I'd give it all, I'd give for us, give anything but I won't give up.
'Cause you know, you know, you know.
(To Chorus:)

SOAK UP THE SUN

Recorded by Sheryl Crow

Words and Music by
SHERYL CROW and JEFF TROTT
Arranged by Richard Bradley

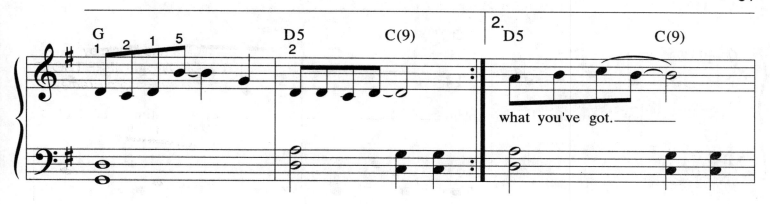

Chorus:

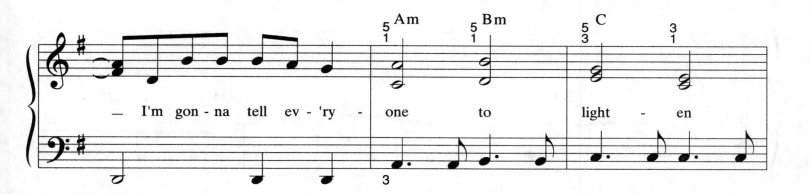

52

THIS I PROMISE YOU

Recorded by 'NSYNC

Words and Music by
RICHARD MARX
Arranged by Richard Bradley

This I Promise You - 6 - 1

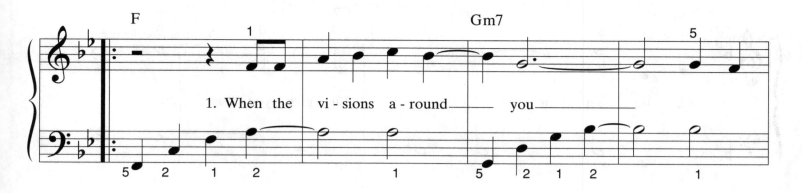

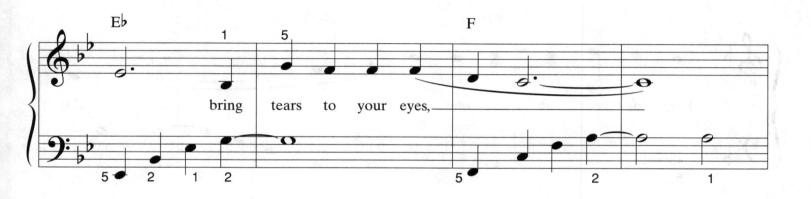

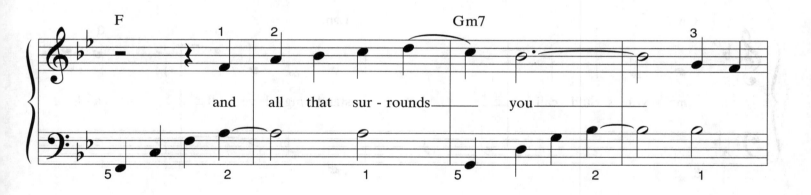

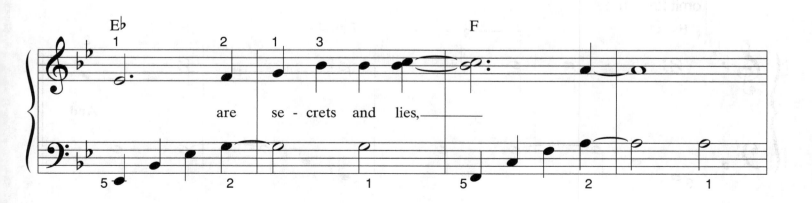

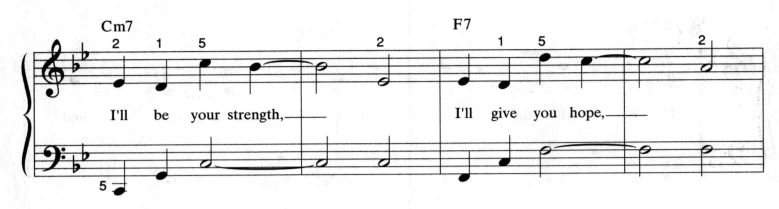

I'll be your strength,— I'll give you hope,—

keep - ing your faith— when it's gone.— The

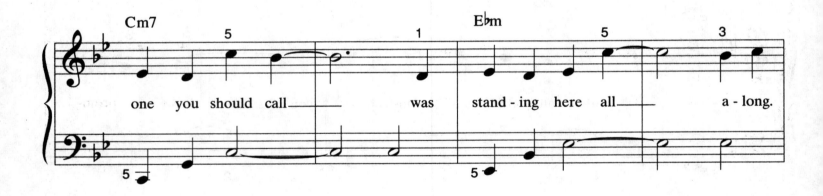

one you should call— was stand - ing here all— a - long.

omit 2nd time

And

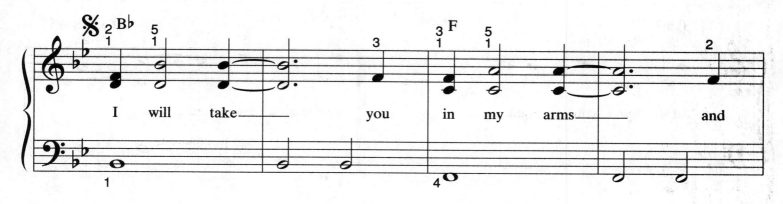

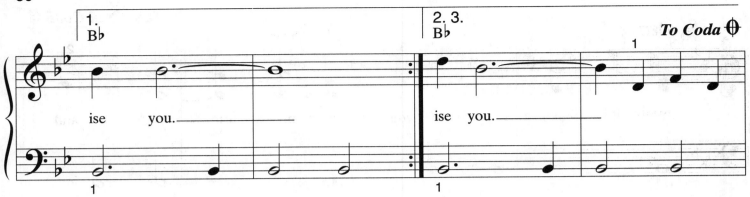

D.S. 𝄋 al Coda ⊕

Coda
⊕

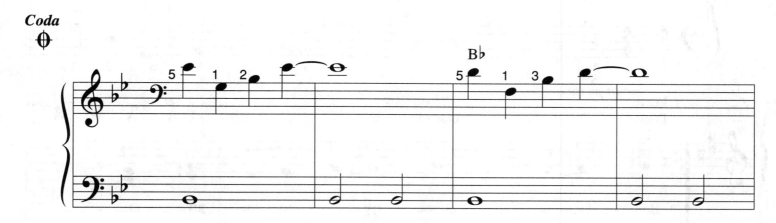

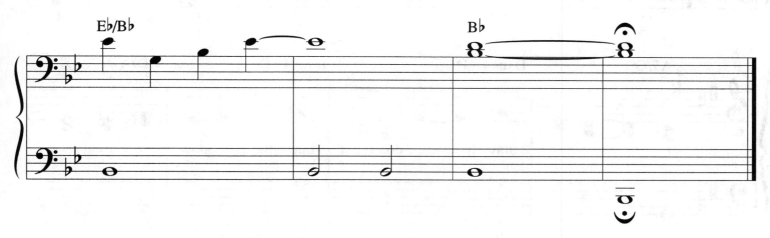

Verse 2:
I've loved you forever in lifetimes before.
And I promise you, never will you hurt anymore.
I give you my word. I give you my heart.
This is the battle I've won.
And with this vow, forever has now begun.
Just close your eyes each loving day
And know this feeling won't go away.

1st time : 'Till the day my life is through,
This I promise you, this I promise you.

2nd time : Every word I say is true,
This I promise you. Ooh, I promise you.

SHAPE OF MY HEART

Recorded by Backstreet Boys

Words and Music by
MAX MARTIN, RAMI
and LISA MISKOVSKY
Arranged by Richard Bradley

Shape of My Heart - 4 - 1

Chorus:

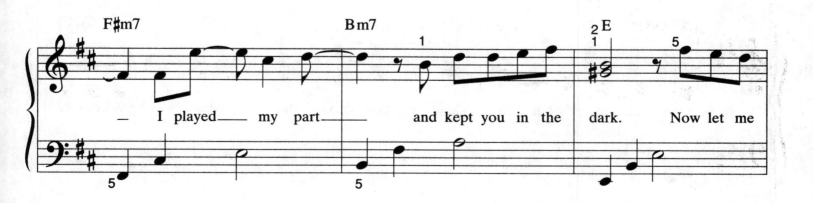

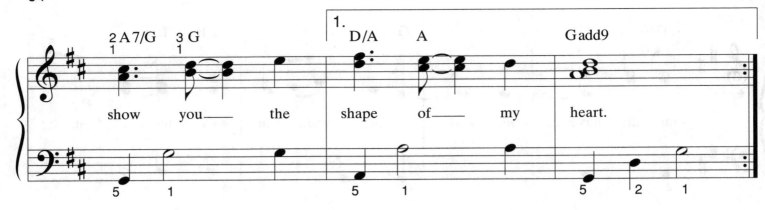

show you the shape of my heart.

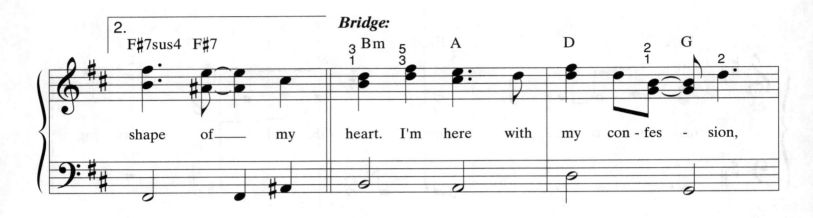

Bridge:

shape of my heart. I'm here with my con - fes - sion,

got noth - ing to hide no more. I don't know where to

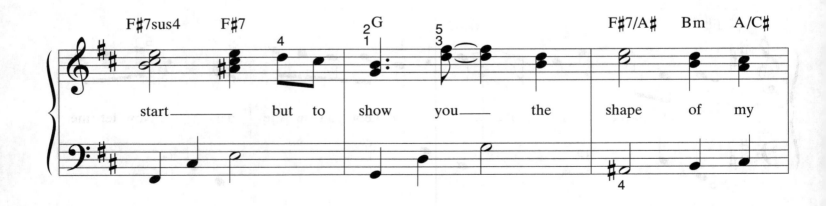

start but to show you the shape of my

Verse 2:
Sadness is beautiful.
Loneliness is tragical.
So help me, I can't win this war.
Touch me now,
Don't bother if every second makes me weaker,
You can save me from the man that I've become.
Oh, yeah. Looking. . .
(To Chorus:)

CAN'T FIGHT THE MOONLIGHT
(THEME FROM "COYOTE UGLY")

Recorded by LeAnn Rimes

Words and Music by
DIANE WARREN
Arranged by Richard Bradley

Can't Fight the Moonlight - 6 - 1

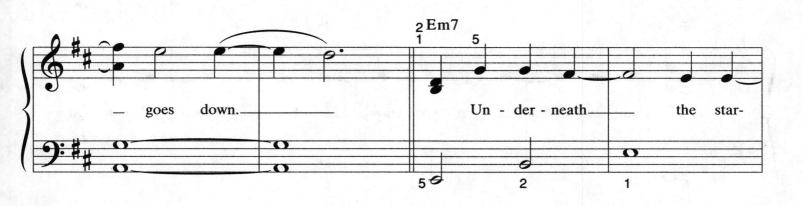

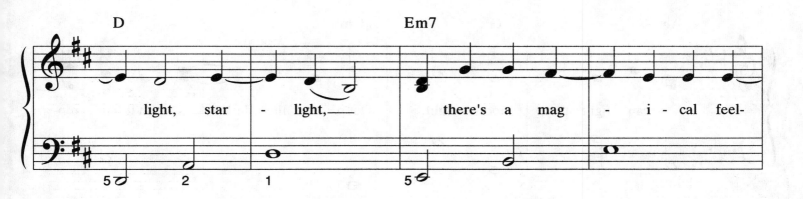

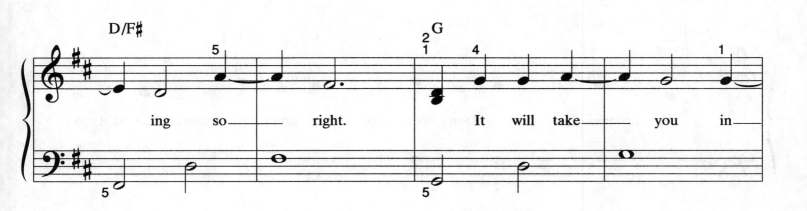

Chorus:

N.C.
Cm

_ to-night. You can try to re-sist____ try to hide

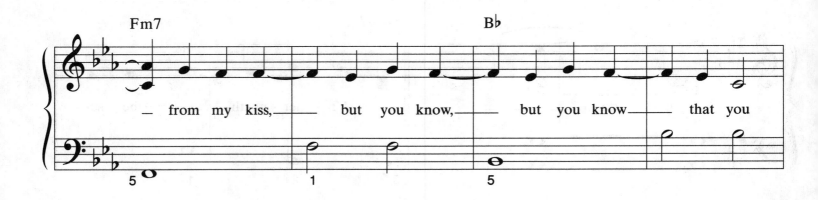

Fm7
B♭

_ from my kiss,____ but you know,____ but you know____ that you

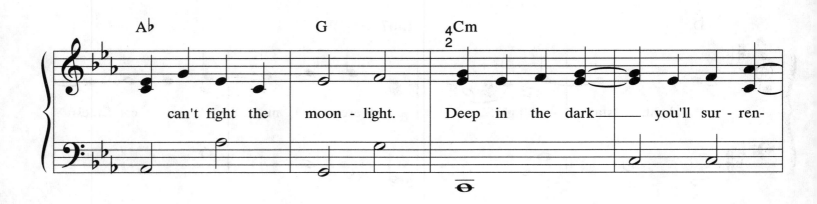

A♭
G
Cm

can't fight the moon-light. Deep in the dark____ you'll sur-ren-

Fm7
B♭

der your heart. Don't you know,____ don't you know____ that you

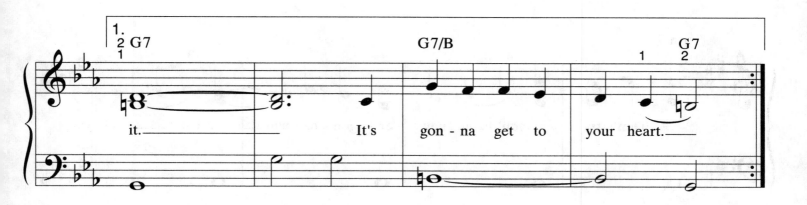

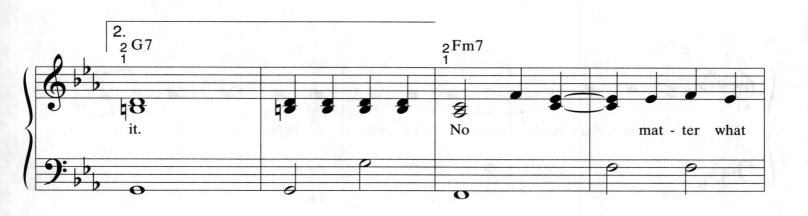

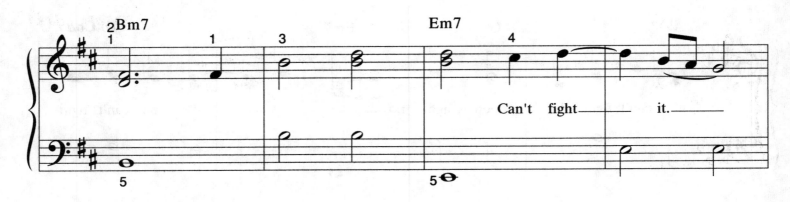

It will steal___ your heart___ to-night.___ You can

Coda

it.___ It's gon-na get to your heart.___

rit.

pp

Verse 2:
There's no escape from love.
Once the gentle breeze
Weaves its spell upon your heart,
No matter what you think,
It won't be too long 'til you're in my arms.
Underneath the starlight, starlight,
We'll be lost in a rhythm so right.
Feel it steal your heart tonight.
You can try . . .
(To Chorus:)

HERO

Recorded by Enrique Iglesias

Words and Music by
ENRIQUE IGLESIAS,
PAUL BARRY and MARK TAYLOR
Arranged by Richard Bradley

in your arms to - night.

Chorus:

I can be your he - ro, ba - by.

I can kiss a - way the pain.

To Coda

I will stand by you for - ev - er.

You can take my breath a - way.

Hero - 6 - 3

Would you

Oh, I just want to hold you.

I just want to hold you, oh, yeah. Am I in too

Verse 3:
Would you swear
That you'll always be mine?
Would you lie?
Would you run and hide?
Am I in too deep?
Have I lost my mind?
I don't care, you're here tonight.

SMOOTH

Recorded by Santana featuring Rob Thomas

Music by ITAAL SHUR and ROB THOMAS
Lyrics by ROB THOMAS
Arranged by Richard Bradley

Moderate Latin feel ♩ = 114

Man, it's a hot one, like sev-en in-ches from the mid-day sun.— Well, I hear you whis-per and the words melt ev-'ry one. But you stay so cool.— My mu-ñe-

qui - ta,   my Span - ish Har - lem Mo - na   Lis - a.

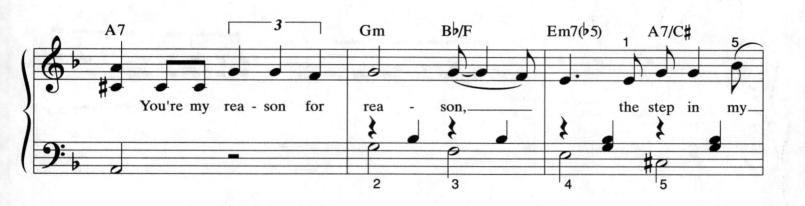

You're my rea - son for rea - son, _____ the step in my __

_ groove.   And if you said ____ this life ain't

good e - nough, ___ I would give my world to lift you up. __ I could

change my life to bet - ter suit___ your___ mood.___

'Cause you're so smooth. Oh, and it's

just like the o - cean un - der the moon.___ Well, it's the same as the e - mo - tion that I

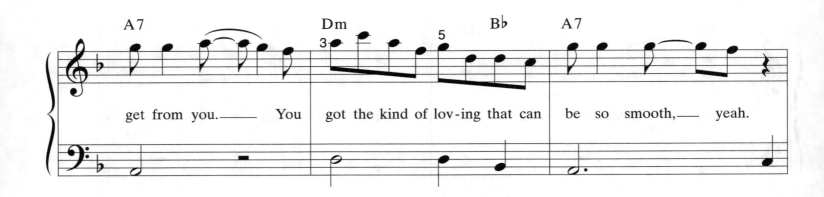

get from you.___ You got the kind of lov-ing that can be so smooth,___ yeah.

Verse 2:
Well, I'll tell you one thing,
If you would leave, it be a crying shame.
In every breath and every word.
I hear your name calling me out, yeah.
Well, out from the barrio,
You hear my rhythm on your radio.
You feel the tugging of the world,
So soft and slow, turning you 'round and 'round.

BIG YELLOW TAXI

Recorded by Counting Crows featuring Vanessa Carlton

Words and Music by
JONI MITCHELL
Arranged by Richard Bradley

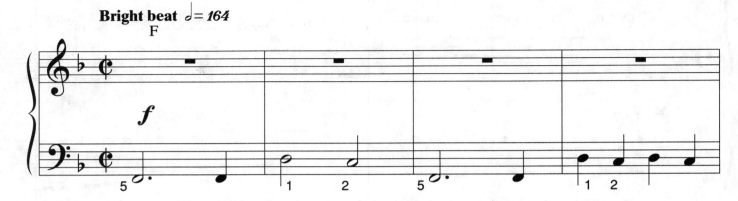

Big Yellow Taxi - 4 - 1

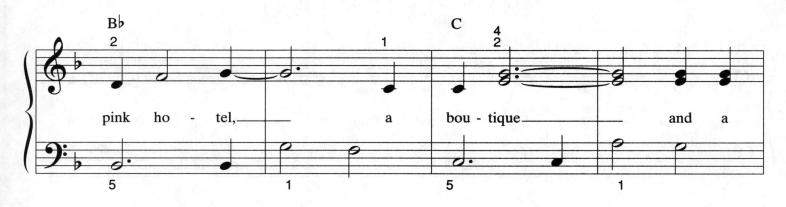

pink ho - tel,_____ a bou - tique_____ and a

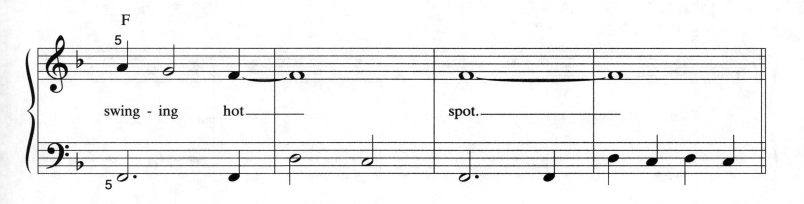

swing - ing hot_____ spot._____

Chorus:

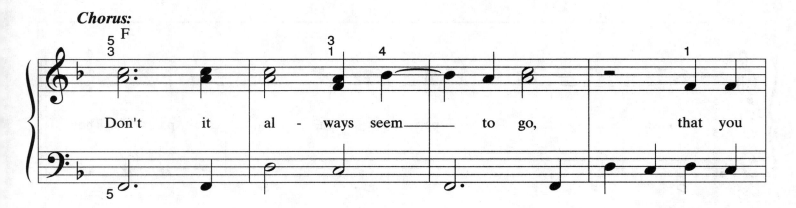

Don't it al - ways seem_____ to go, that you

don't know what_____ you've got_____ till it's gone? They

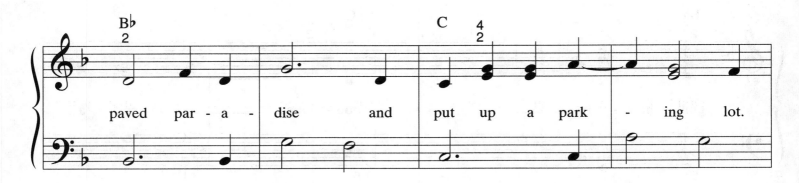

paved par - a - dise   and   put up a park - ing lot.

1. 2. 3.

Woo,   pa,   pa, pa,   pa.

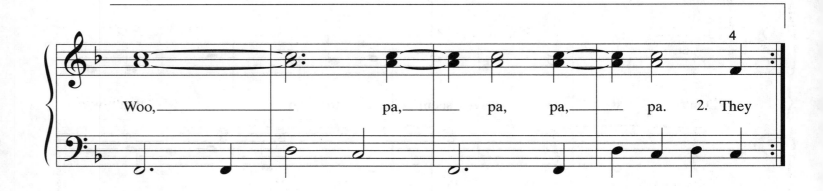

Woo,   pa,   pa, pa,   pa.   2. They

4.

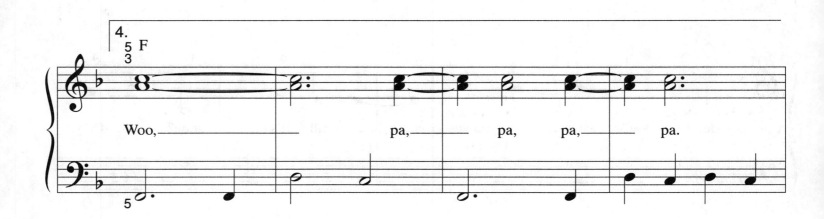

Woo,   pa,   pa, pa,   pa.

Don't it al - ways seem to go, _____ that you

don't know what _____ you've got _____ till it's gone? They

paved par - a - dise and put up a park - ing lot.

Woo, _____ pa, _____ pa, pa _____ pa.

Repeat and fade

Verse 2:
They took all the trees
And put them in a tree museum,
And they charged all the people
A dollar and a half just to see them.
(To Chorus:)

Verse 3:
Hey, farmer, farmer,
Put away that D.D.T. now,
Give me spots on my apples
But leave me the birds and the bees,
Please!
(To Chorus:)

Verse 4:
Late, late last night
I heard the screen door slam,
And a big yellow taxi
Took away my old man.
(To Chorus:)

BREAKAWAY

Recorded by Kelly Clarkson

Words and Music by
MATTHEW GERRARD, AVRIL LAVIGNE,
and BRIDGET BENENATE
Arranged by Richard Bradley

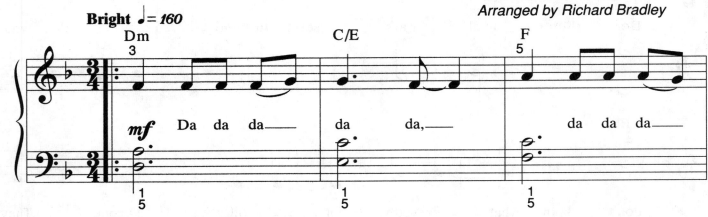

Verse:

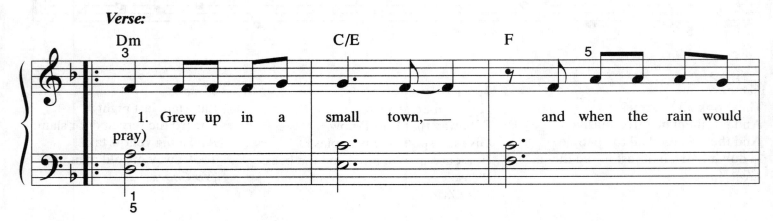

Breakaway - 6 - 1

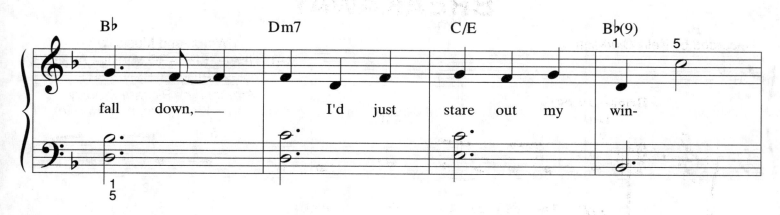

fall down,___ I'd just stare out my win-

dow, dream-in' of what could be,___ and if I'd end up

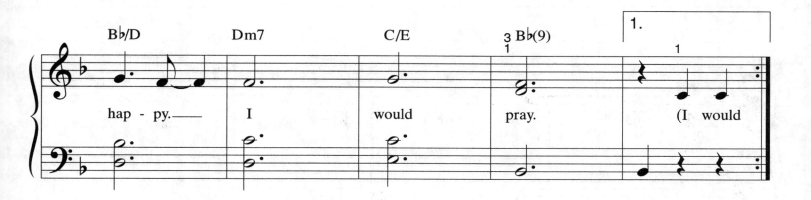

hap - py.___ I would pray. (I would

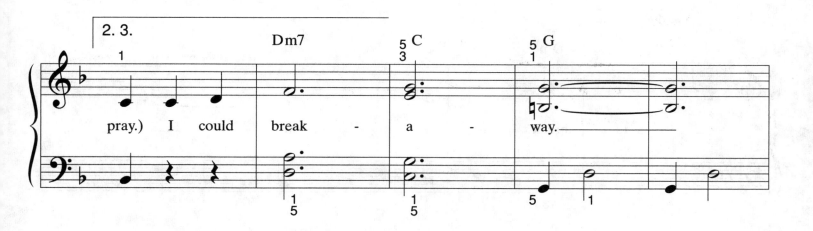

pray.) I could break - a - way.___

I'll spread my wings and I'll learn how to

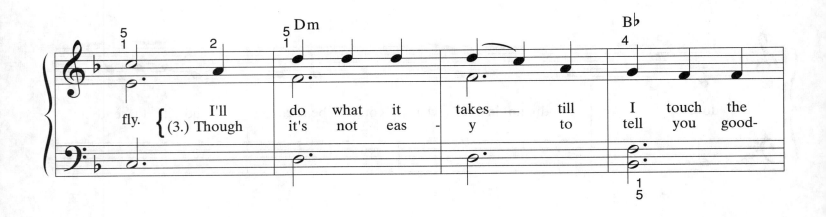

fly. { (3.) Though } I'll do what it takes till I touch the
it's not eas - y to tell you good-

sky. And I'll make a wish, } take a chance, make a change,
bye, got - ta take a risk, }

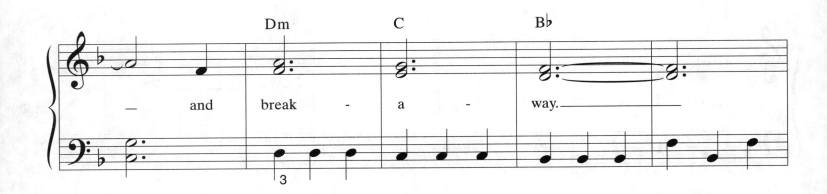

— and break - a - way.

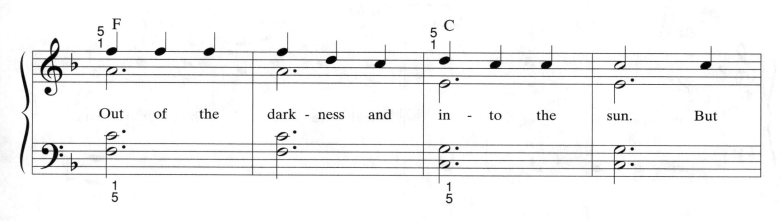

Out of the dark - ness and in - to the sun. But

I won't for - get { all the ones that I love, }
{ the place I come from. } I'll

To Coda ⊕

take a risk, take a chance, make a change ___ and

D.C.

break - a - way. ___

Bridge:

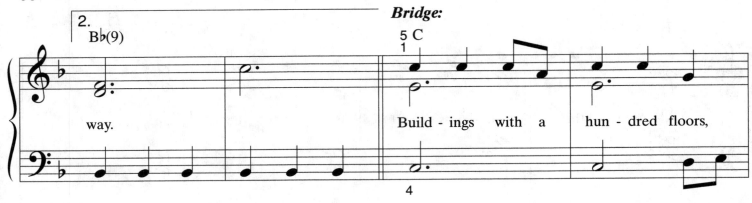

way.   Build - ings   with   a   hun - dred floors,

swing - in' 'round re - volv - ing   doors.   May - be   I   don't

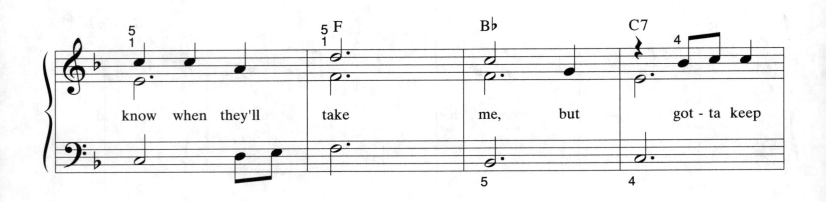

know   when they'll   take   me,   but   got - ta keep

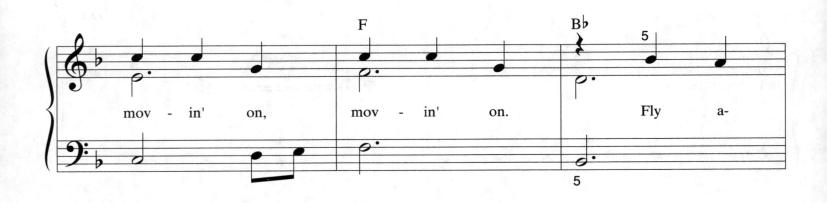

mov - in'   on,   mov - in'   on.   Fly a-

Verse 2:
Trying hard to reach out,
But when I tried to speak out,
Felt like no one could hear me.
Wanted to belong here,
But something felt so wrong here.
So I pray (I would pray.)
I could breakaway.
(To Chorus:)

Verse 3:
Wanna feel the warm breeze,
Sleep under a palm tree,
Feel the rush of the ocean.
Get on board a fast train,
Travel on a jet plane,
Far away and breakaway.
(To Chorus:)

THEME FROM ICE CASTLES
(THROUGH THE EYES OF LOVE)

From the Motion Picture *Ice Castles*
Academy Award Nominee - Best Song
Recorded by Melissa Manchester

Lyrics by CAROL BAYER SAGER
Music by MARVIN HAMLISCH
Arranged by Richard Bradley

Please, don't let this feel-ing end. It's ev - 'ry thing I
now I can take the time. I can see my

am, it's ev - 'ry thing I want to be. I can see what's
life as it comes up shin - ing now. Reach - ing out to

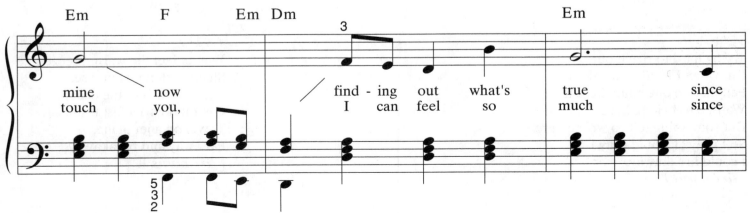

mine now find - ing out what's true since
touch you, I can feel so much since

Theme from Ice Castles - 4 - 1

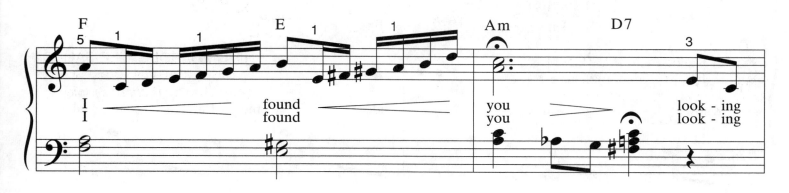

Theme from Ice Castles - 4 - 2

PLATOON SWIMS

Composed by
CLINT EASTWOOD
Arranged by Richard Bradley

From the Motion Picture *Flags of Our Fathers*

THE NOTEBOOK
(MAIN TITLE)

From the Motion Picture *The Notebook*
Winner, BMI Film Music Award

Written by
AARON ZIGMAN
Arranged by Richard Bradley

BECAUSE YOU LOVED ME

Theme from *Up Close & Personal*
Academy Award Nominee - Best Song
Recorded by Celine Dion

Words and Music by
DIANE WARREN
Arranged by Richard Bradley

For all— those times you stood— by me, for all— the

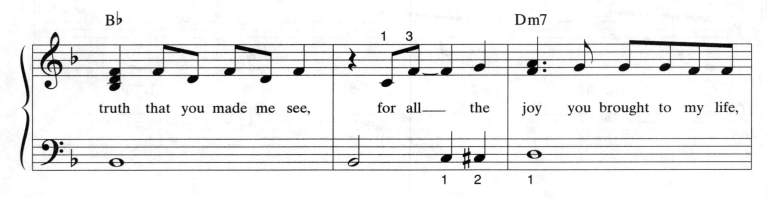

truth that you made me see, for all— the joy you brought to my life,

for all— the wrong that you— made right, for ev - ery—

dream you made— come true, for all— the love I found— in you,—

I'll be for - ev - er thank - ful, ba - by.

You're the one who held me up, nev-er let me fall.

You're the one who saw me through, through it all.

You were my strength when I was weak, you were my

Verse 2:
You gave me wings and made me fly,
You touched my hand, I could touch the sky.
I lost my faith, you gave it back to me.
You said no star was out of reach,
You stood by me and I stood tall.
I had your love, I had it all.
I'm grateful for each day you gave me.
Maybe I don't know that much,
But I know this much is true.
I was blessed because I was loved by you.

I DON'T WANT TO MISS A THING

From the Motion Picture *Armageddon*
Academy Award Nominee - Best Song
Recorded by Aerosmith

Words and Music by
DIANE WARREN
Arranged by Richard Bradley

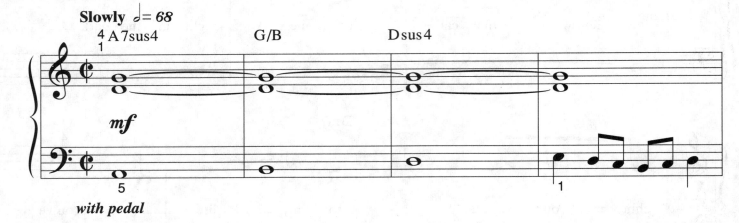

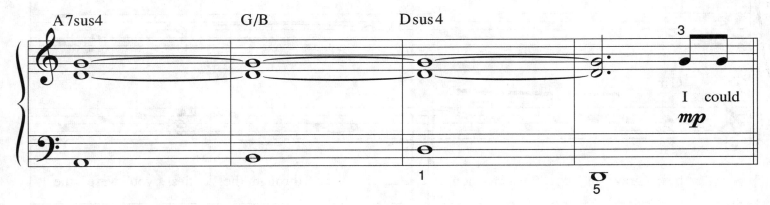

stay a-wake   just to hear you   breath - ing,_____   watch you

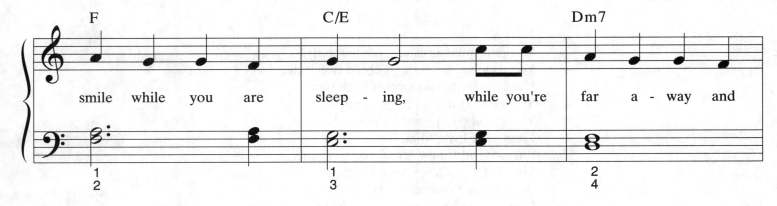

smile   while   you   are   sleep - ing,   while you're   far a - way   and

I Don't Want to Miss a Thing - 5 - 1

Verse 2:
Laying close to you, feeling your heart beating,
And I'm wondering what you're dreaming,
Wondering if it's me you're seeing.
Then I kiss your eyes and thank God we're together.
I just wanna stay with you in this moment together.

THE ROSE

From the Motion Picture *The Rose*
Recorded by Bette Midler

Words and Music by
AMANDA McBROOM
Arranged by Richard Bradley

The Rose - 3 - 1

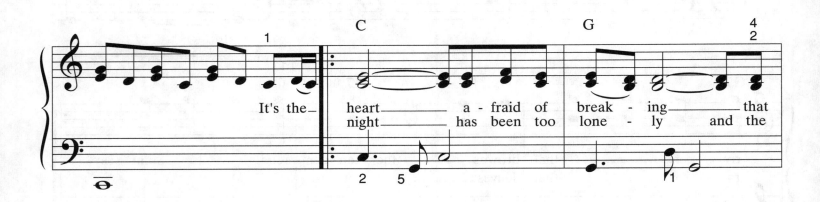

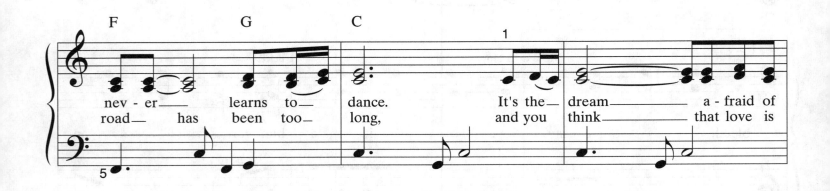

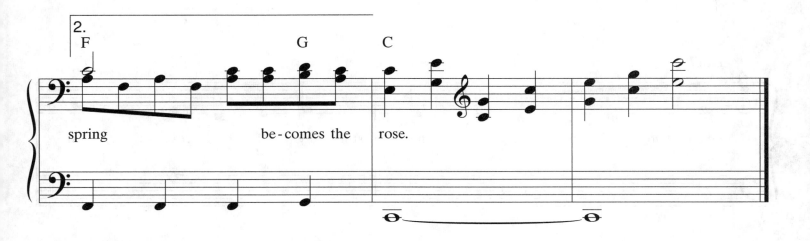

The Rose - 3 - 3

AS TIME GOES BY

From the Motion Picture *Casablanca*.
Performed in the film by Dooley Wilson

Words and Music by
HERMAN HUPFELD
Arranged by Richard Bradley

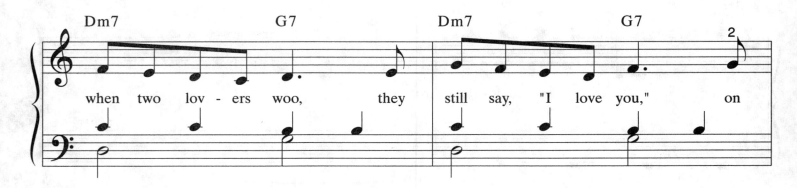

As Time Goes By - 4 - 1

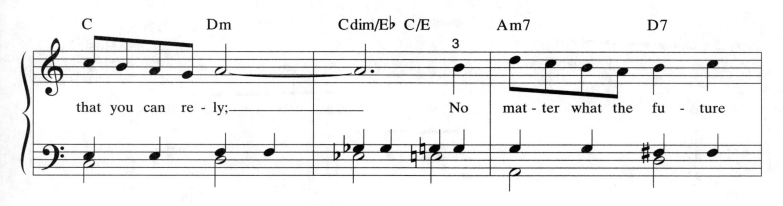

that you can re - ly; No mat - ter what the fu - ture

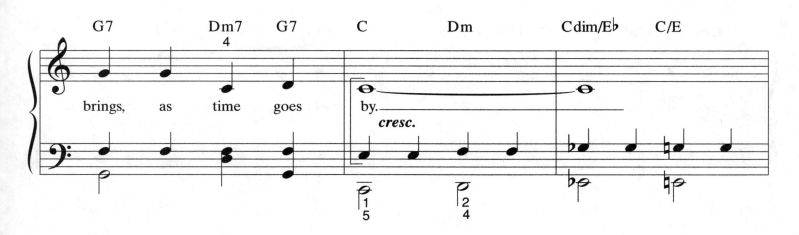

brings, as time goes by.

cresc.

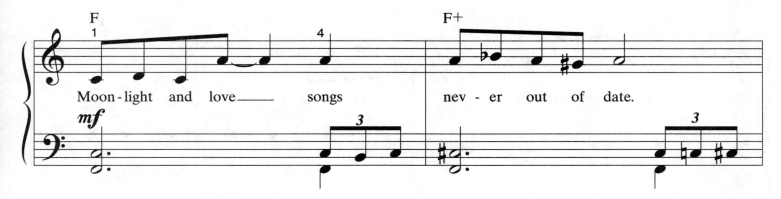

Moon - light and love songs nev - er out of date.

mf

Hearts full of pas - sion, jeal - ous - y and hate;

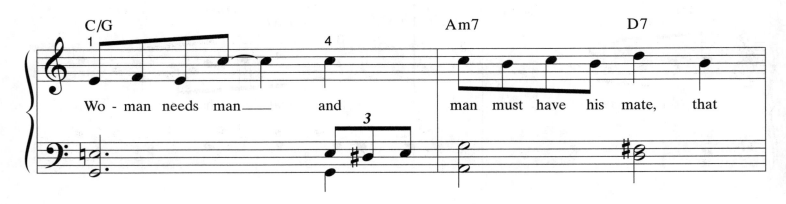

Wo - man needs man—— and man must have his mate, that

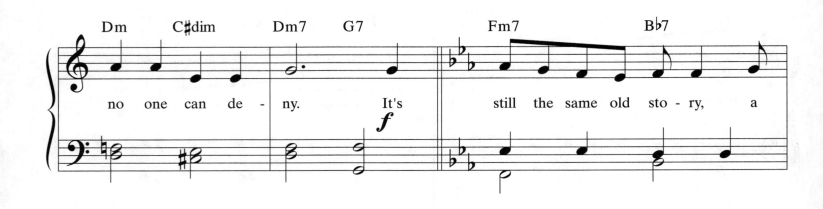

no one can de - ny. It's still the same old sto - ry, a

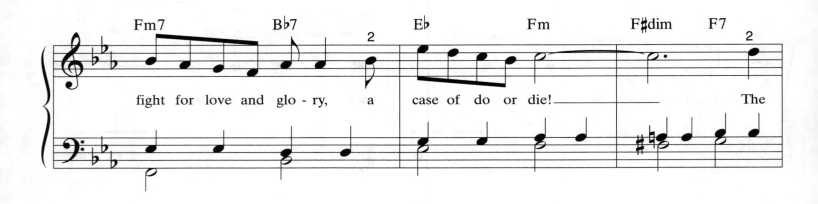

fight for love and glo - ry, a case of do or die!———— The

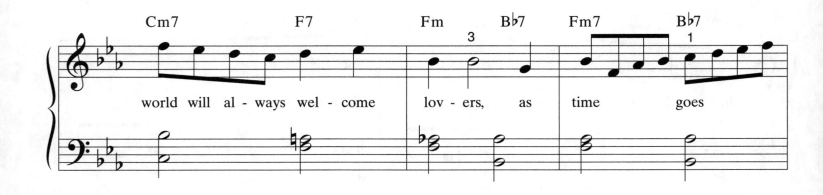

world will al - ways wel - come lov - ers, as time goes

OVER THE RAINBOW

From the Motion Picture *The Wizard of Oz*
Sung by Judy Garland
Academy Award Winner - Best Song

Lyric by E.Y. HARBURG
Music by HAROLD ARLEN
Arranged by Richard Bradley

Over the Rainbow - 3 - 1

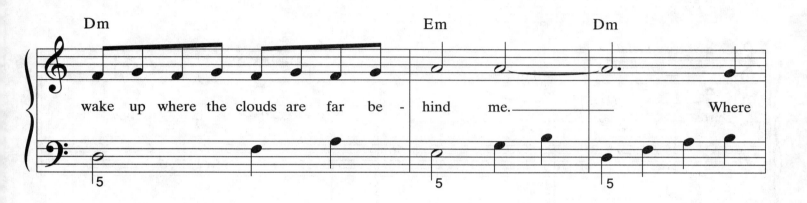

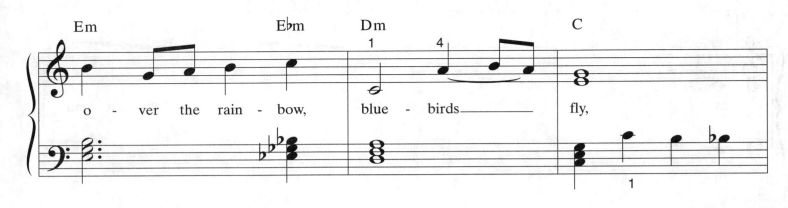

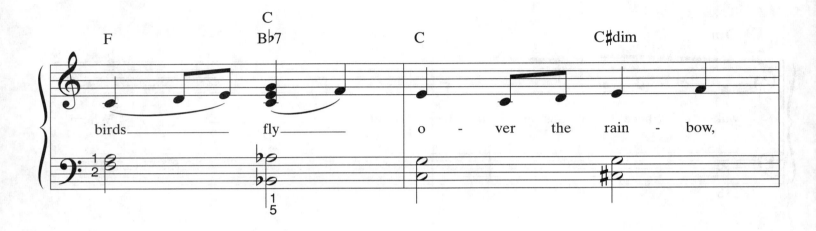

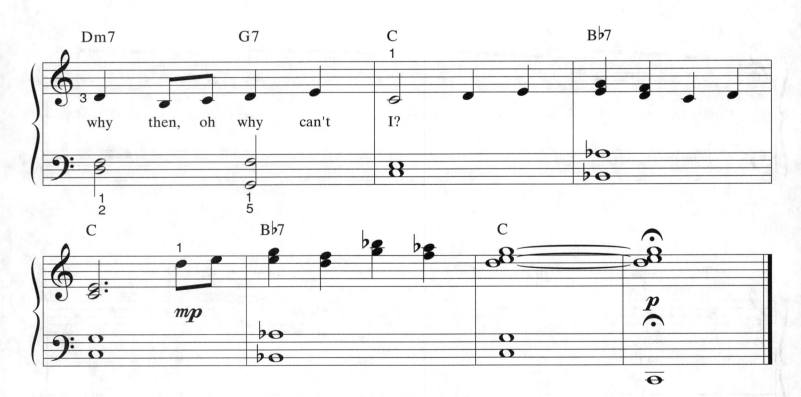

SINGIN' IN THE RAIN

From the Motion Picture *Singin' in the Rain*
Sung by Gene Kelly

Lyric by ARTHUR FREED
Music by NACIO HERB BROWN
Arranged by Richard Bradley

Lyrics: I'm sing - in' in the rain, just sing - in' in the rain. What a glo - ri - ous feel - ing, I'm hap - py a - gain. I'm

Singin' in the Rain - 3 - 1

laugh - ing at clouds so dark up a-

bove. The sun's in my heart, and I'm

read - y for love. Let the storm - y clouds

chase ev - 'ry - one from the place. Come

THE PINK PANTHER

From the Motion Picture *The Pink Panther*
Academy Award Nominee - Best Score

Music by
HENRY MANCINI
Arranged by Richard Bradley

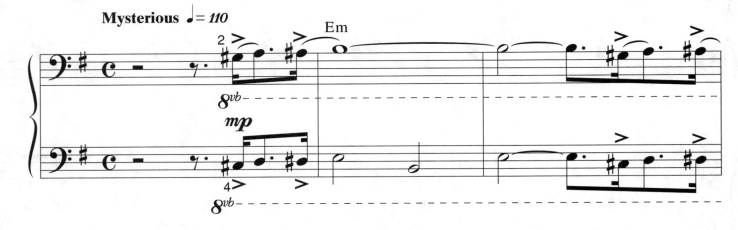

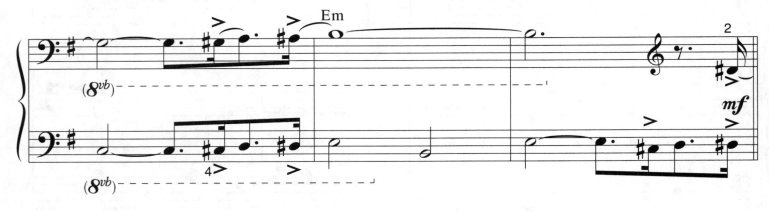

The Pink Panther - 3 - 1

126

Opening Theme from

MARCH OF THE PENGUINS
(THE HARSHEST PLACE ON EARTH)

By
ALEX WURMAN
Arranged by Richard Bradley

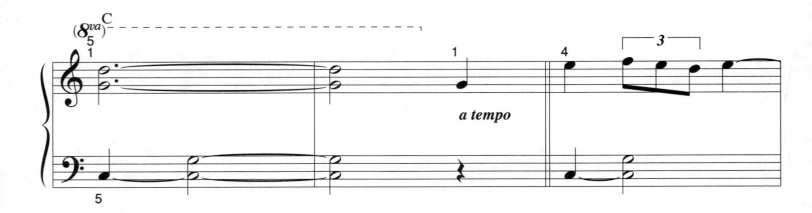

March of the Penguins - 4 - 5

WONKA'S WELCOME SONG

From the Motion Picture
Charlie and the Chocolate Factory

Music by DANNY ELFMAN
Lyrics by JOHN AUGUST and DANNY ELFMAN
Arranged by Richard Bradley

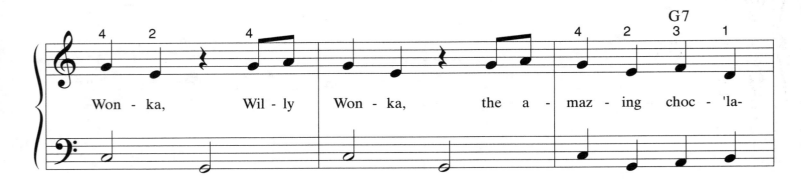

Wonka's Welcome Song - 1 - 4

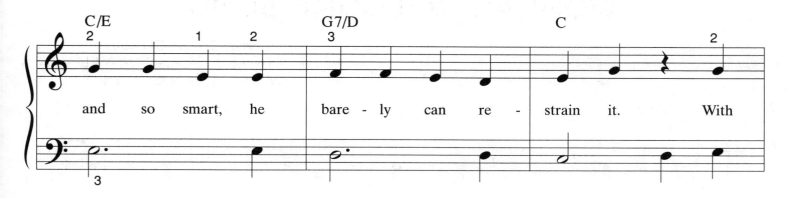

and so smart, he bare - ly can re - strain it. With

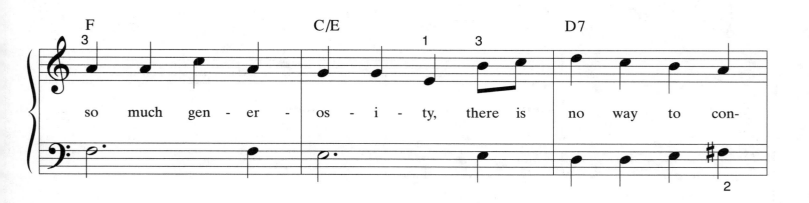

so much gen - er - os - i - ty, there is no way to con-

tain it, to con - tain it, to con - tain, to con - tain, to con-

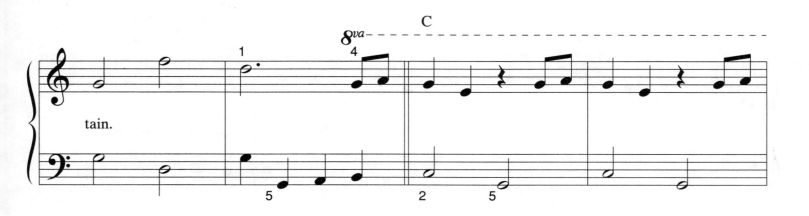

tain.

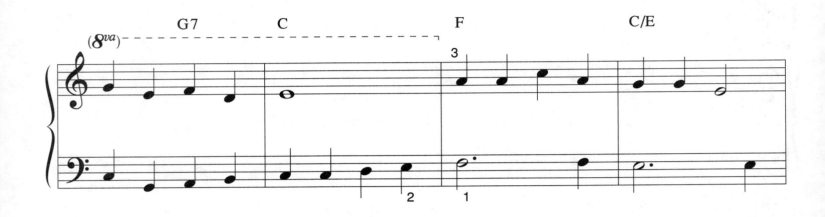

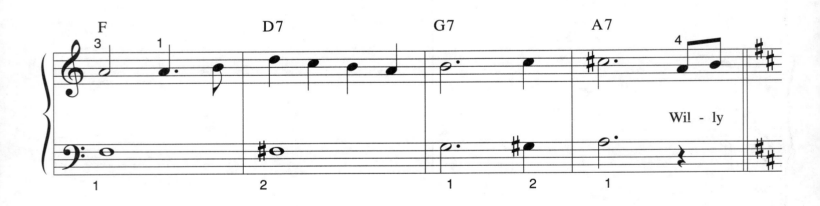

STAR WARS (MAIN TITLE)

From the Motion Picture *Star Wars*
Academy Award Winner - Best Score

Music by
JOHN WILLIAMS
Arranged by Richard Bradley

I GOT A NAME

From the Motion Pictures
The Last American Hero (1973)
and *Invincible* (2006)
Sung in both by Jim Croce

Words by NORMAN GIMBEL
Music by CHARLES FOX
Arranged by Richard Bradley

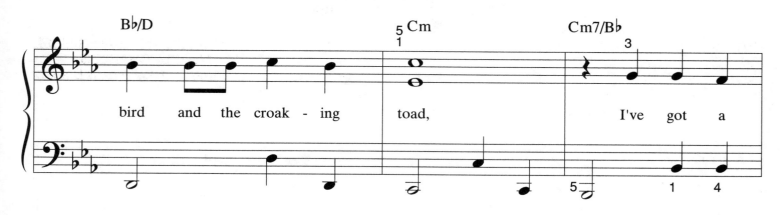

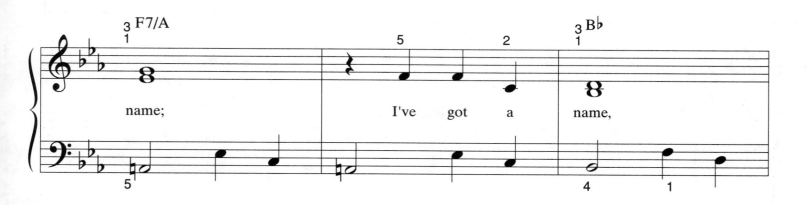

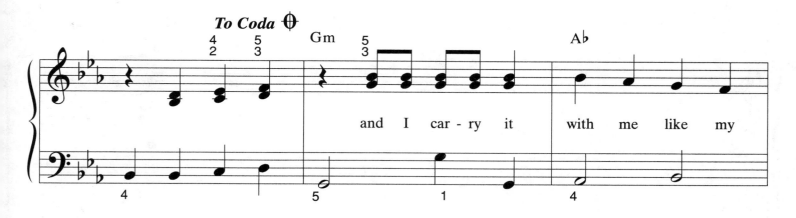

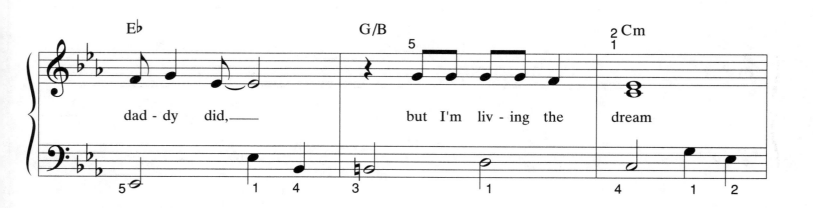

I Got a Name - 2 - 5

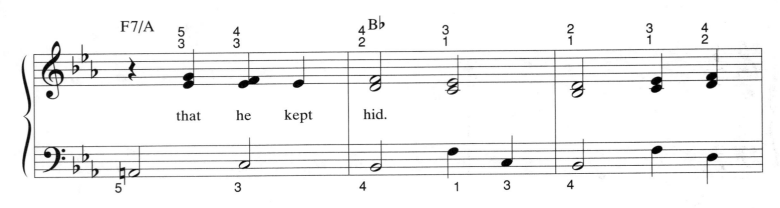

that he kept hid.

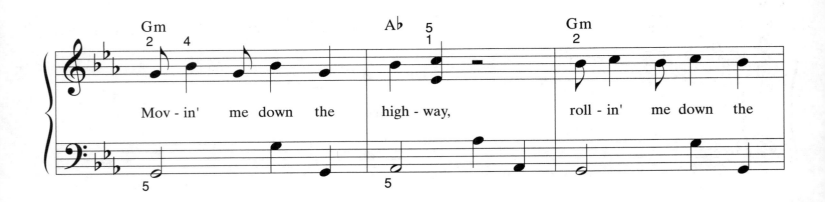

Mov-in' me down the high-way, roll-in' me down the

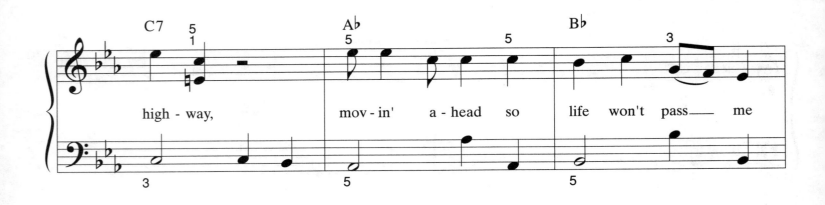

high-way, mov-in' a-head so life won't pass____ me

by.____

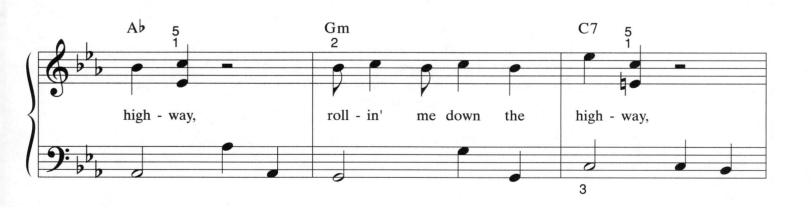

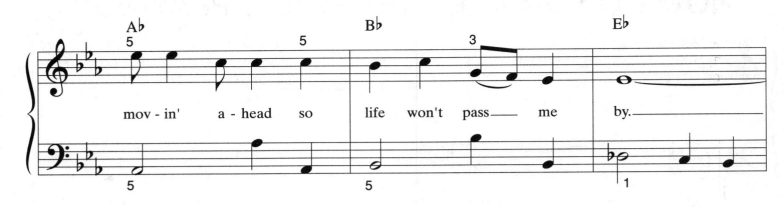

mov - in' a - head so life won't pass___ me by.___

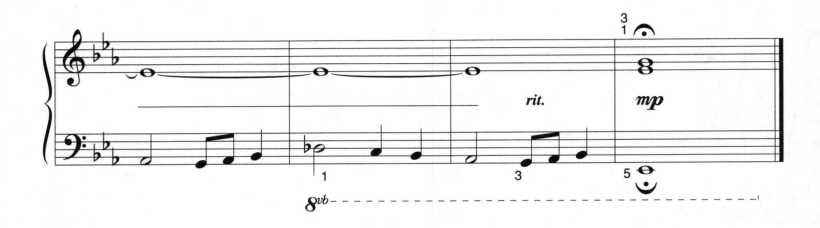

rit.

mp

Verse 2:
Like the north wind whistlin' down the sky,
I've got a song; I've got a song.
Like the whipoorwill and the baby's cry,
I've got a song; I've got a song.
And I carry it with me and I sing it loud;
If it gets me nowhere, I'll go there proud.

Verse 3:
(Instrumental)

Verse 4:
Like the fool I am and I'll always be,
I got a dream; I got a dream.
They can change their minds but they can't change me,
I've got a dream; I've got a dream.
Oh, I know I could share it if you'd want me to;
If you're goin' my way, I'll go with you.

HOW DO YOU KEEP THE MUSIC PLAYING?

From the Motion Picture *Best Friends*
Academy Award Nominee - Best Song
Recorded by Patti Austin and James Ingram

Words by ALAN and MARILYN BERGMAN
Music by MICHEL LEGRAND
Arranged by Richard Bradley

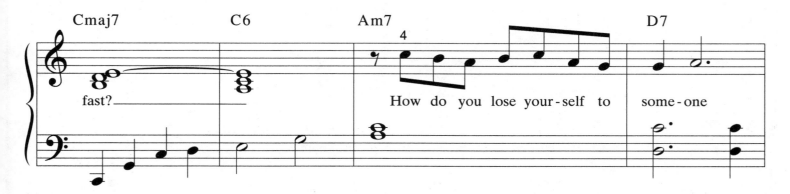

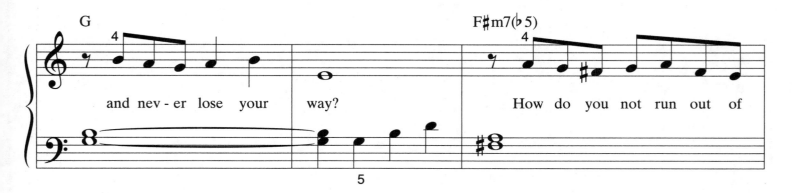

How Do You Keep the Music Playing? - 3 - 1

144

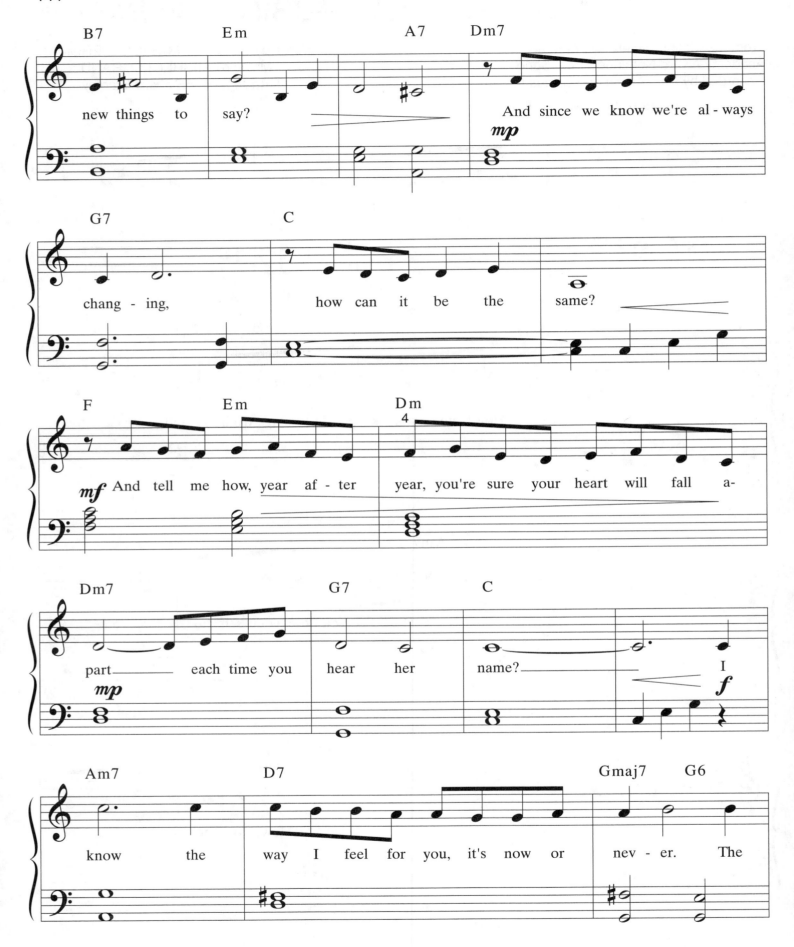

HOW DO I LIVE

From the Motion Picture *Con Air*
Academy Award Nominee - Best Song
Soundtrack Recording by Trisha Yearwood
Popular Recording by LeAnn Rimes

Words and Music by
DIANE WARREN
Arranged by Richard Bradley

Moderately slow ♩ = 84

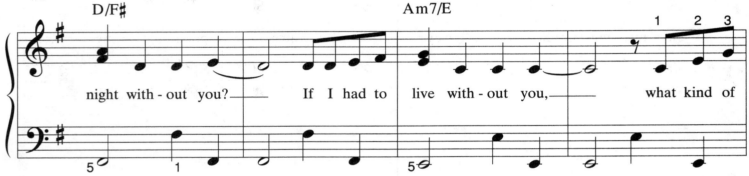

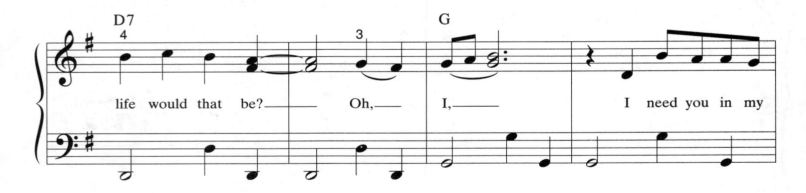

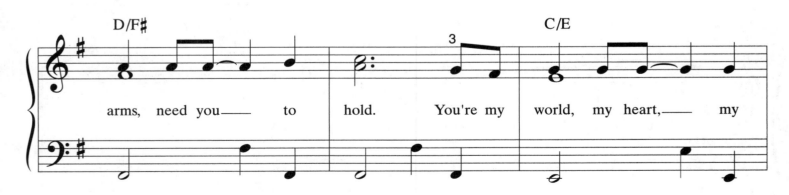

How Do I Live - 5 - 1

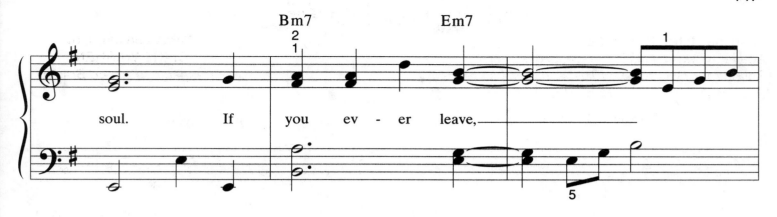

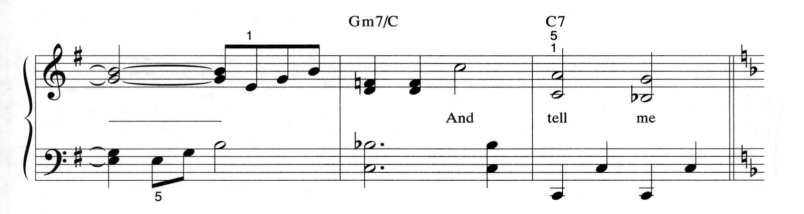

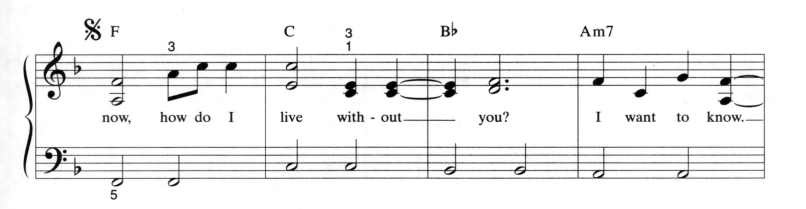

How Do I Live - 5 - 2

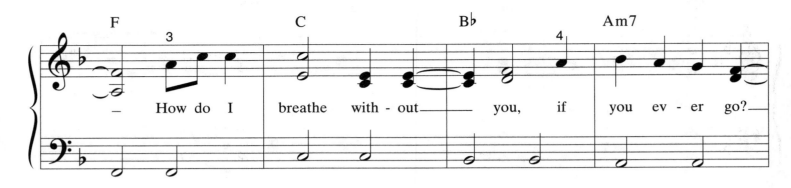

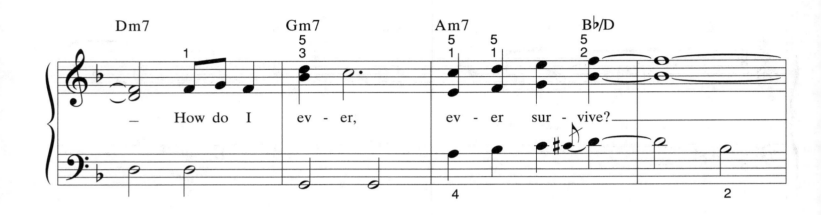

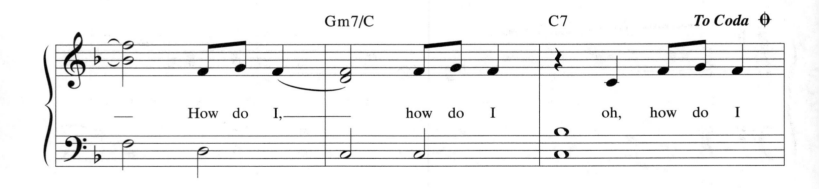

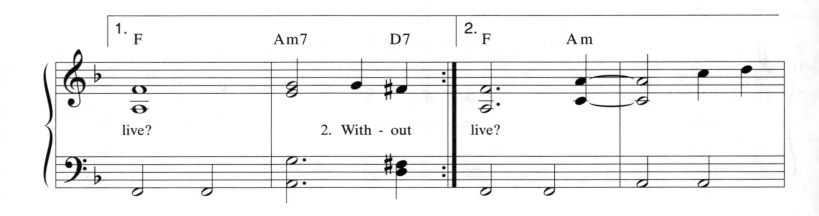

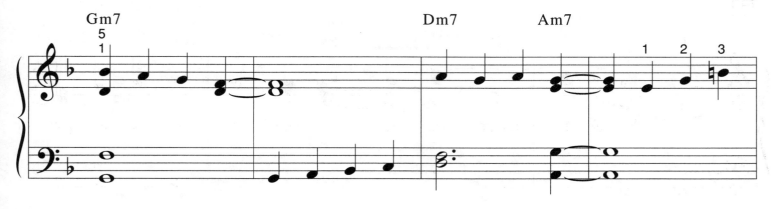

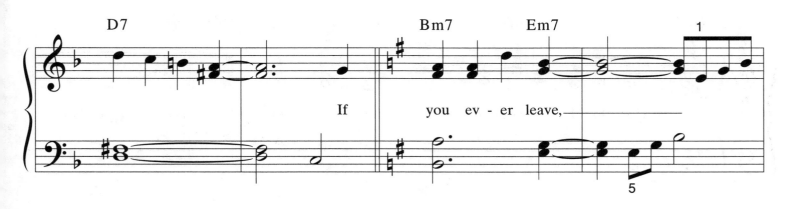

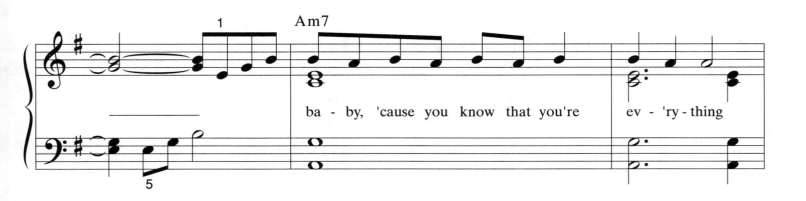

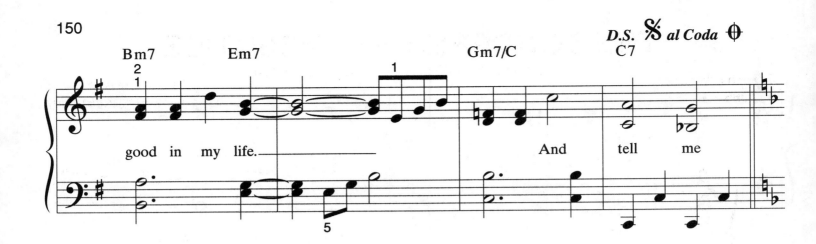

good in my life.___ And tell me

Coda ⊕

live with - out

you?

Verse 2:
Without you, there'd be no sun in my sky,
There would be no love in my life,
There'd be no world left for me.
And I, baby, I don't know what I would do,
I'd be lost if I lost you.
If you ever leave,
Baby, you would take away everything real in my life,
And tell me now. . .
(To Chorus:)

THE SORCERER'S APPRENTICE

Used in the Motion Picture *Walt Disney's Fantasia*

French composer
1865 – 1935

PAUL DUKAS
Arranged by Richard Bradley

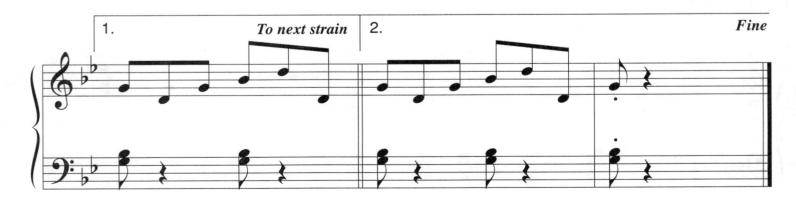

ALSO SPRACH ZARATHUSTRA

Used as the theme for the Motion Picture *2001: A Space Odyssey*

German composer
1864 – 1949

RICHARD STRAUSS
Arranged by Richard Bradley

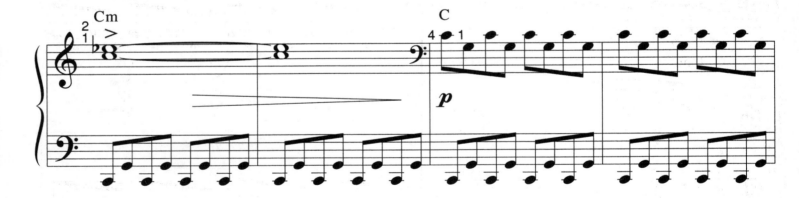

Also Sprach Zarathustra - 2 - 1

WILLIAM TELL OVERTURE

Italian composer
1792 – 1868

GIOACCHINO ROSSINI
Arranged by Richard Bradley

with pedal

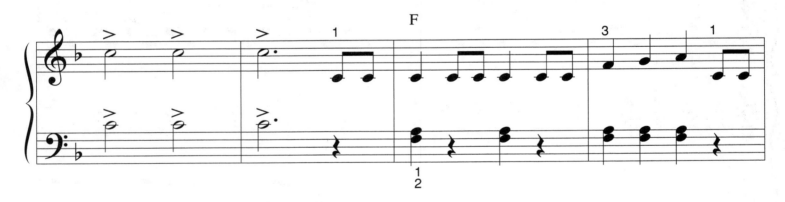

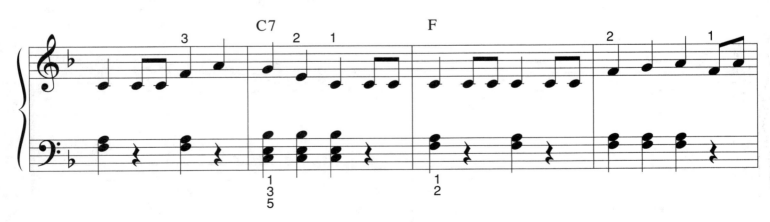

William Tell Overture - 4 - 1

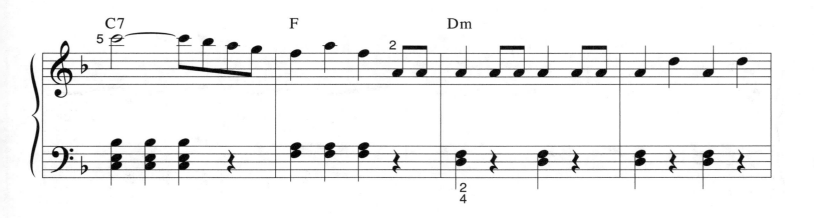

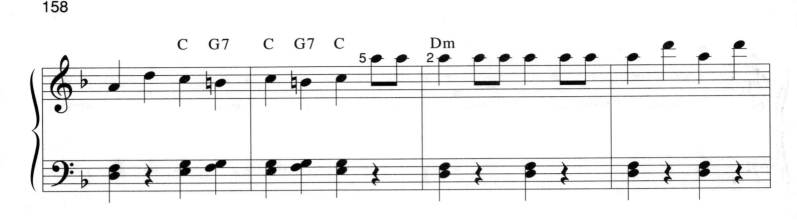

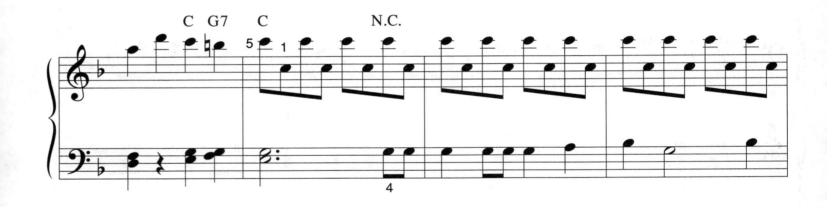

FÜR ELISE
(MAIN THEME)

German composer
1770 – 1827

LUDWIG van BEETHOVEN
Edited by Richard Bradley

Für Elise - 2 - 1

CLAIR DE LUNE
(FIRST THEME)

French composer
1862 – 1918

CLAUDE DEBUSSY
Arranged by Richard Bradley

Clair de Lune - 2 - 1

MOONLIGHT SONATA
(Op. 27, No. 2)

German composer
1770 – 1827

LUDWIG van BEETHOVEN
Arranged by Richard Bradley

Moonlight Sonata - 4 - 1

UN BEL DÌ

From the opera *Madame Butterfly*

Italian composer
1858 – 1924

GIACOMO PUCCINI
Arranged by Richard Bradley

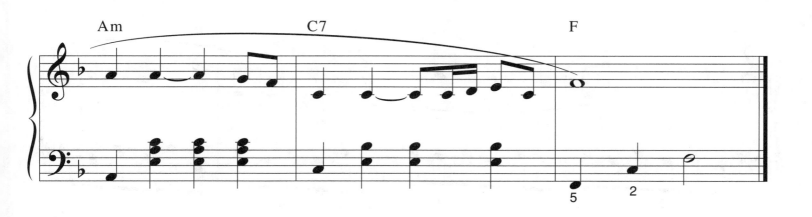

LULLABY

German composer
1833 – 1897

JOHANNES BRAHMS
Arranged by Richard Bradley

Lullaby - 2 - 1

NORWEGIAN DANCE

Norwegian composer
1843 – 1907

EDVARD GRIEG
Arranged by Richard Bradley

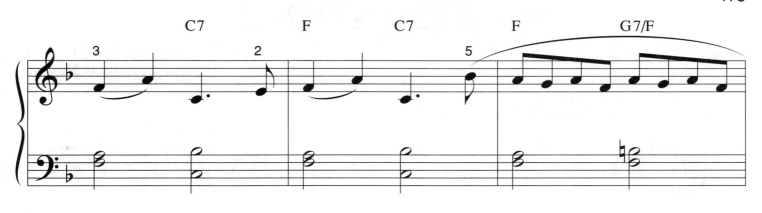

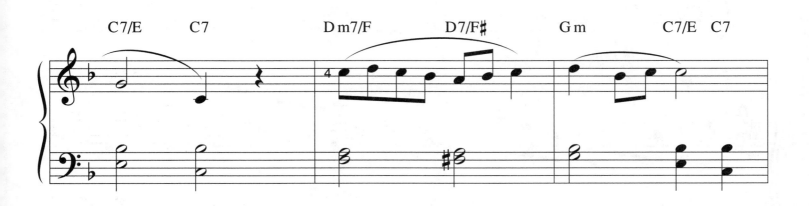

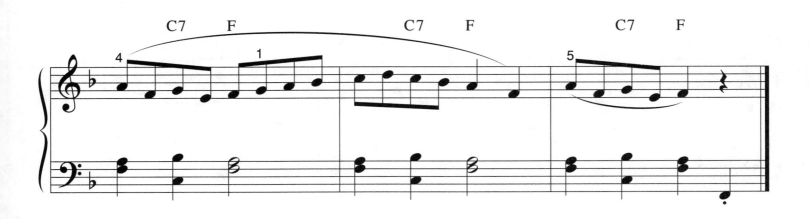

CANON IN D

Used as the theme for the Motion Picture *Ordinary People*

German organist - composer
1653 – 1706

JOHANN PACHELBEL
Arranged by Richard Bradley

Canon in D - 4 - 2

177

Canon in D - 4 - 4

HUNGARIAN RHAPSODY NO. 2

Hungarian pianist - composer
1811 – 1886

FRANZ LISZT
Arranged by Richard Bradley

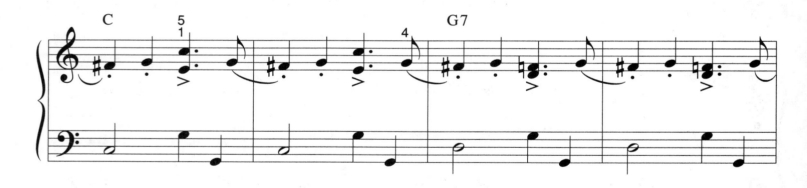

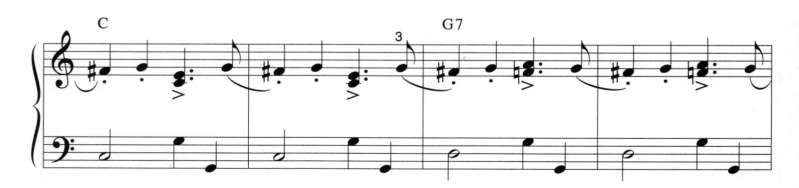

THE FLIGHT OF THE BUMBLE-BEE

Russian composer
1844 – 1908

NIKOLAY RIMSKY-KORSAKOV
Arranged by Richard Bradley

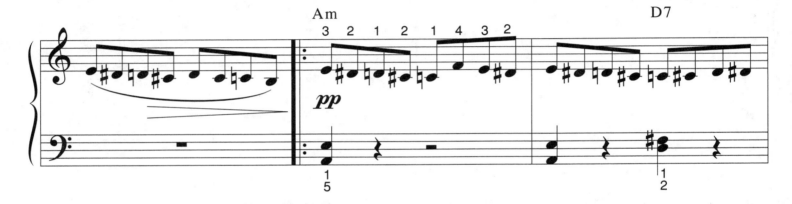

The Flight of the Bumble-Bee - 4 - 1

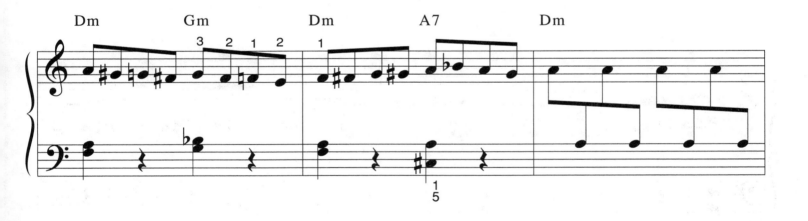

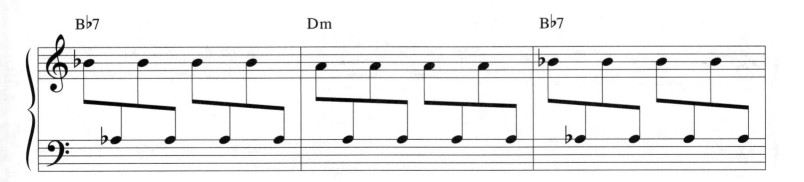

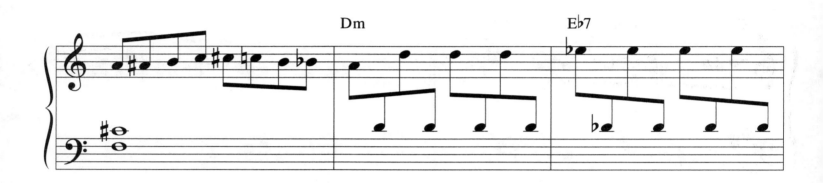

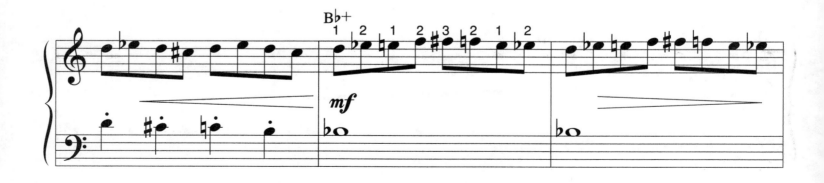

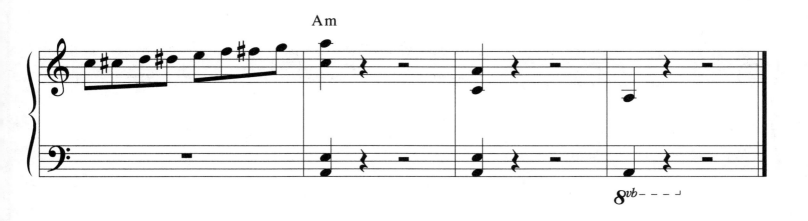

The Flight of the Bumble-Bee - 4 - 4

FUNERAL MARCH OF THE MARIONETTES

Used as the theme for the TV series *Alfred Hitchcock Presents*

French composer
1818 – 1893

CHARLES GOUNOD
Arranged by Richard Bradley

Funeral March of the Marionettes - 2 - 1

THEME FROM
SWAN LAKE

Russian composer
1840 - 1893

PETER ILYICH TCHAIKOVSKY
Arranged by Richard Bradley

Theme from Swan Lake - 3 - 1

Theme from Swan Lake - 3 - 2

SONG FROM M*A*S*H

Theme from the Television Series *M*A*S*H*

Words and Music by
MIKE ALTMAN and JOHNNY MANDEL
Arranged by Richard Bradley

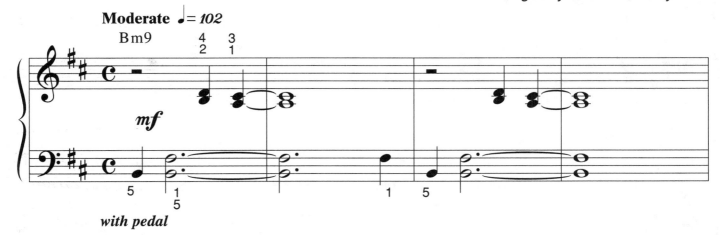

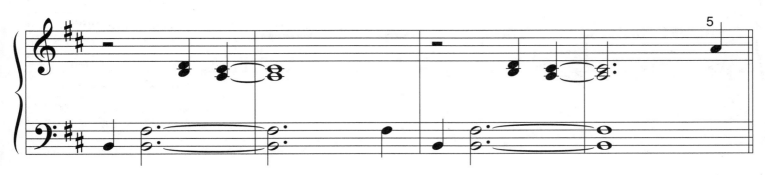

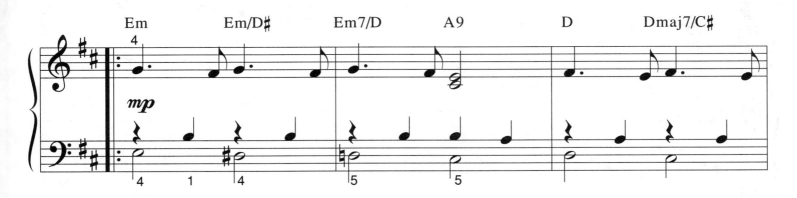

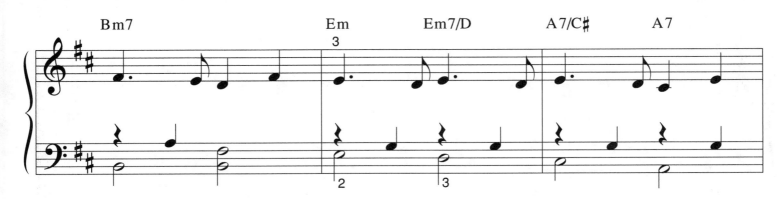

Song from M*A*S*H - 3 - 1

190

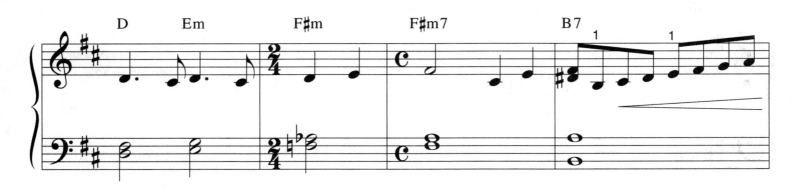

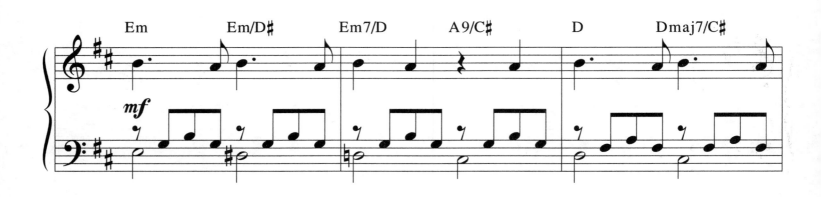

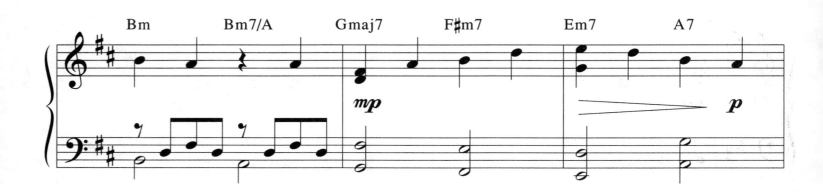

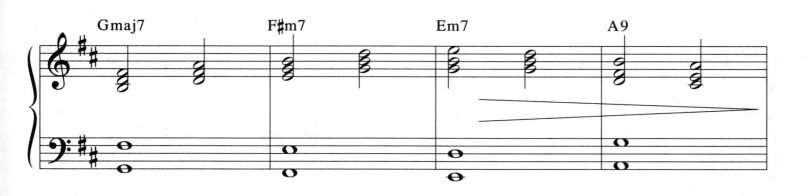

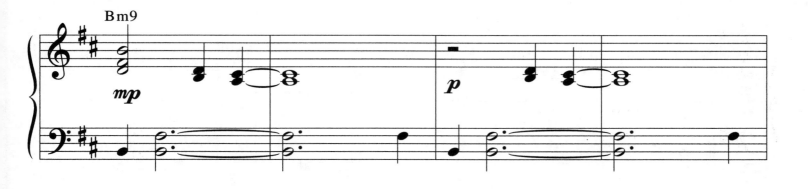

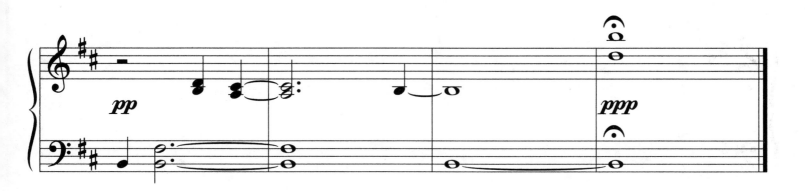

Song from M*A*S*H - 3 - 3

THE WEST WING
(MAIN TITLE)

From the TV Series *The West Wing*

Composed by
W. G. SNUFFY WALDEN
Arranged by Richard Bradley

The West Wing - 2 - 1

The West Wing - 2 - 2

CALIFORNIA

From Warner Bros. Television's *The O.C.*
Recorded by Phantom Planet

Words and Music by
AL JOLSON, B.G. DESYLVA, JOSEPH MEYER,
JASON SCHWARTZMAN and ALEX GREENWALD
Arranged by Richard Bradley

Moderately slow rock ♩ = *80*

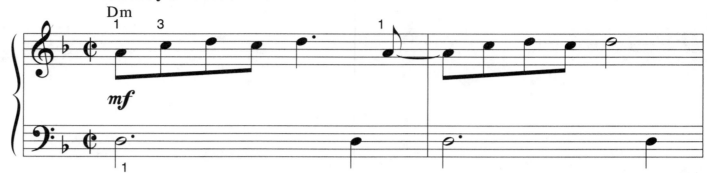

1. We've been on the run, driv - ing in the sun,
2. On the ste - re - o, lis - ten as we go,

California - 1 - 7

look - ing out for num - ber one.
noth - ing's gon - na stop me now.
Cal - i - for-

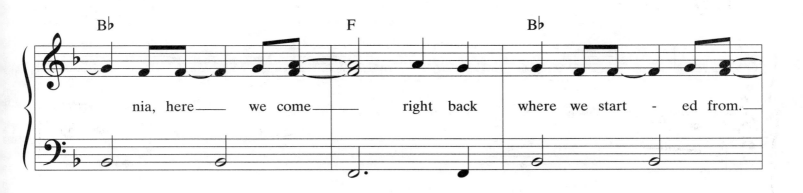

nia, here we come right back where we start - ed from.

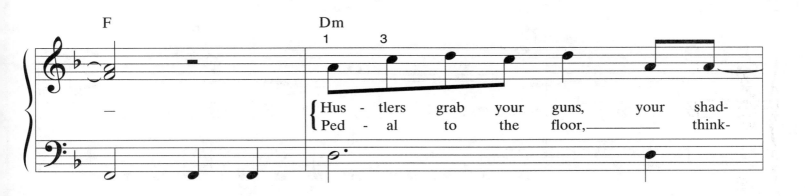

Hus - tlers grab your guns, your shad-
Ped - al to the floor, think-

ow weighs a ton, driv - ing down the 1 - 0 - 1.
in' of the roar, got - ta get us to the show.

Cal - i - for - nia, here___ we come,___ right back

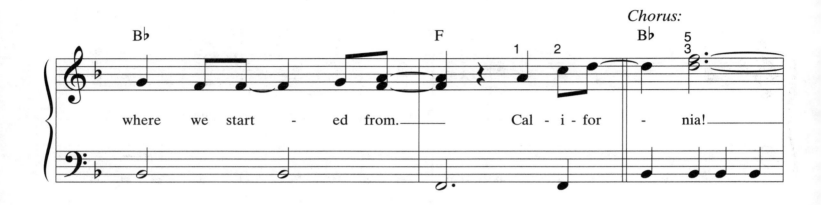

where we start - ed from.___ Cal - i - for - nia!___

Chorus:

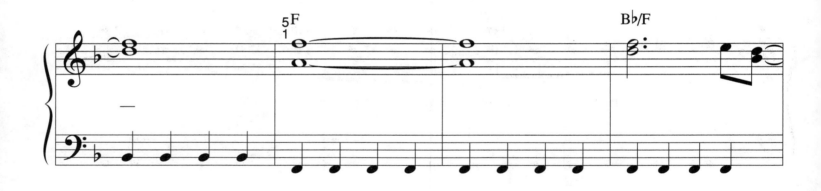

Here,___ we come!___

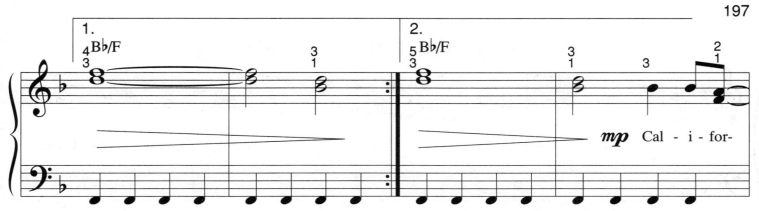

California - 4 - 7

BOSS OF ME

Theme from the TV Series *Malcolm in the Middle*
Recorded by They Might Be Giants

Words and Music by
JOHN FLANSBURGH
and JOHN LINNELL
Arranged by Richard Bradley

You're not the boss of me now. You're not the boss of me now.

You're not the boss of me now, and you're not so big.

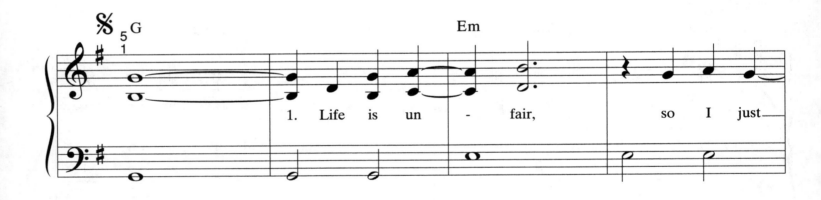

1. Life is un - fair, so I just

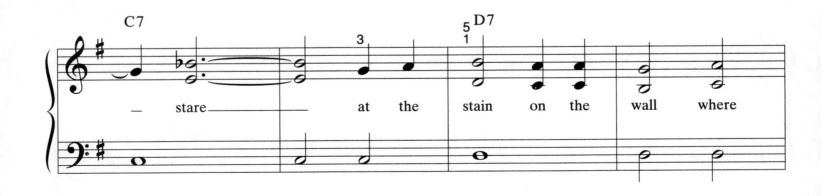

stare at the stain on the wall where

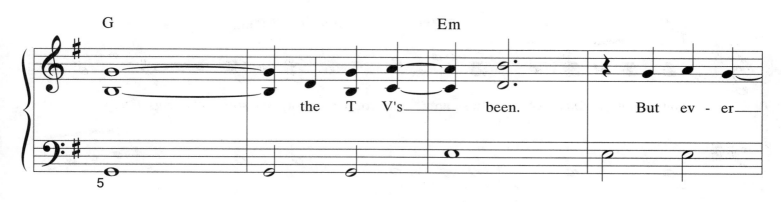

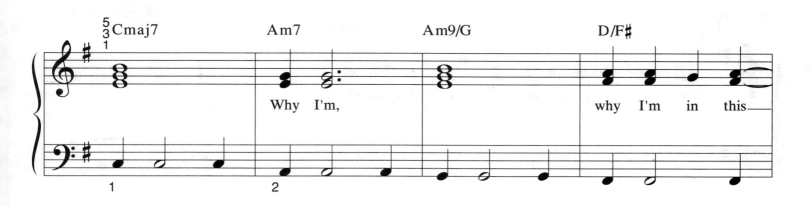

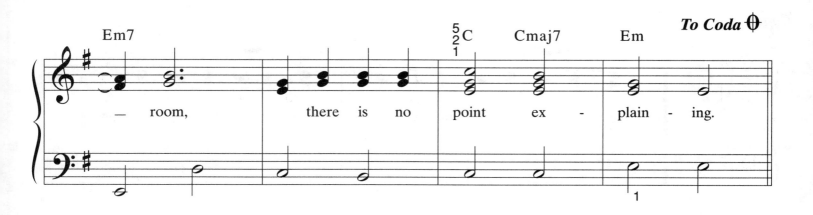

Boss of Me - 5 - 3

Coda

Verse 2:
Life is a test, but I confess
I like this mess I've made so far.
Grade on a curve, and you'll observe
I'm right below the horizon.
Yes, no, maybe, I don't know,
Can you repeat the question?

EVERYBODY LOVES RAYMOND
(MAIN TITLE)

From the TV Series *Everybody Loves Raymond*

Words and Music by
RICK MAROTTA
and TERRY TROTTER
Arranged by Richard Bradley

KING OF THE HILL

From the Twentieth Century Fox TV Series *King Of The Hill*

Words and Music by
ROGER CLYNE, BRIAN BLUSH,
ARTHUR EDWARDS and PAUL NAFFAH
Arranged by Richard Bradley

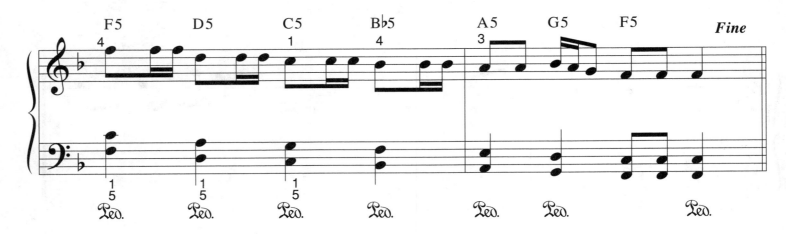

King of the Hill - 2 - 1

ER
(MAIN THEME)

From the TV Series *ER*

Composed by
JAMES NEWTON HOWARD
Arranged by Richard Bradley

ER - 2 - 1

ER - 2 - 2

24
(END TITLE THEME)

From the TV Series *24*

Composed by
SEAN CALLERY
Arranged by Richard Bradley

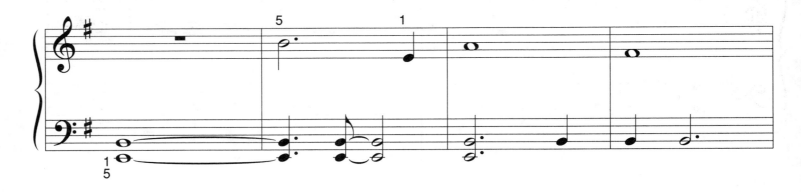

24 (End Title Theme) - 2 - 1

THEME FROM "NYPD BLUE"

From the TV Series *NYPD Blue*

Music by
MIKE POST
Arranged by Richard Bradley

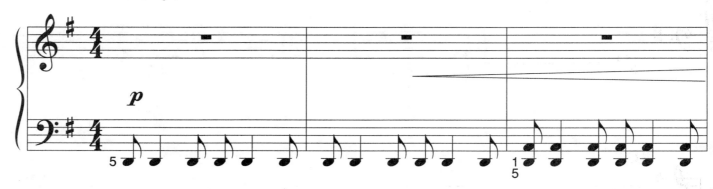

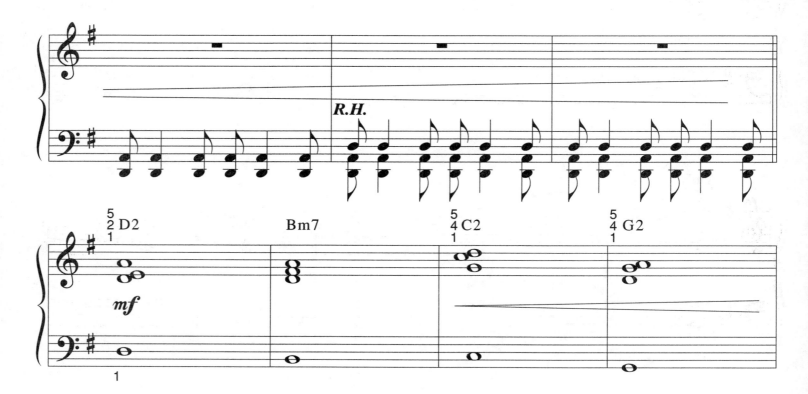

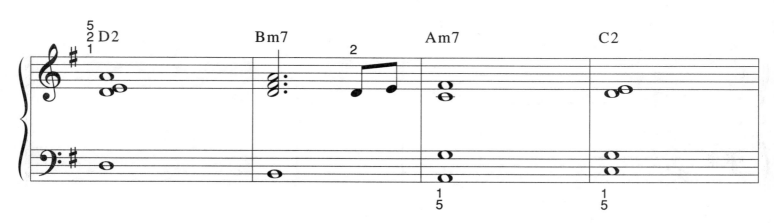

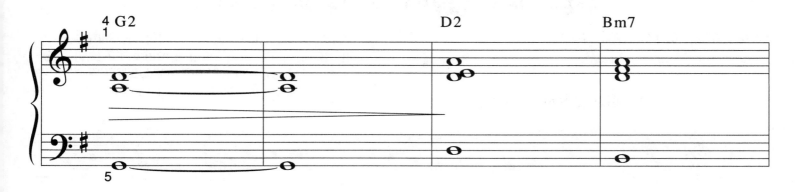

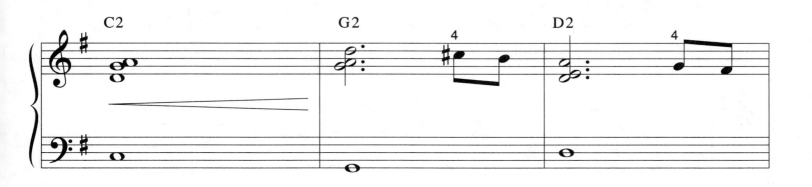

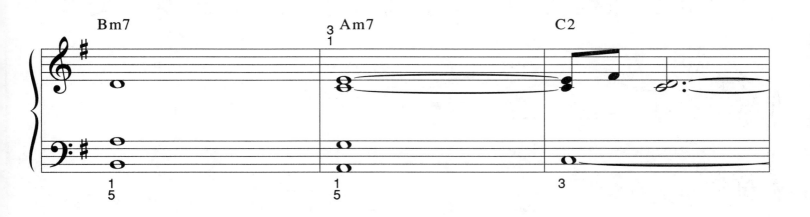

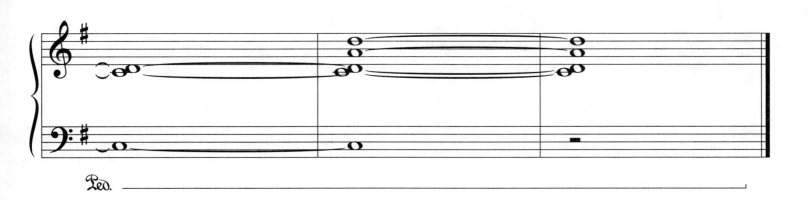

Theme from "NYPD Blue" - 2 - 2

I'LL BE THERE FOR YOU

Theme from the TV Series *Friends*
Recorded by The Rembrandts

Words by DAVID CRANE, MARTA KAUFMAN,
PHIL SOLEM, DANNY WILDE and ALLEE WILLIS
Music by MICHAEL SKLOFF
Arranged by Richard Bradley

So, no — one told you life — was gon-na be — this way.

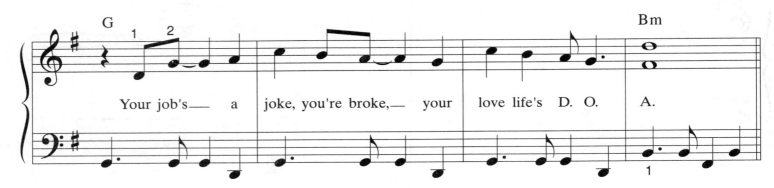

Your job's — a joke, you're broke, — your love life's D. O. A.

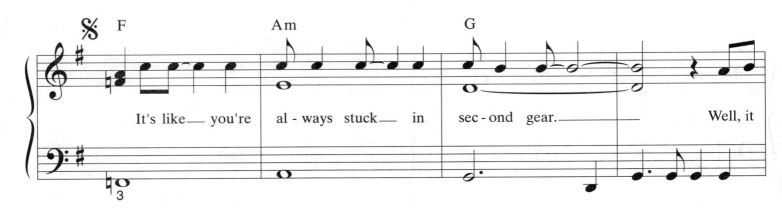

It's like — you're al-ways stuck — in sec-ond gear. — Well, it

I'll Be There for You - 6 - 1

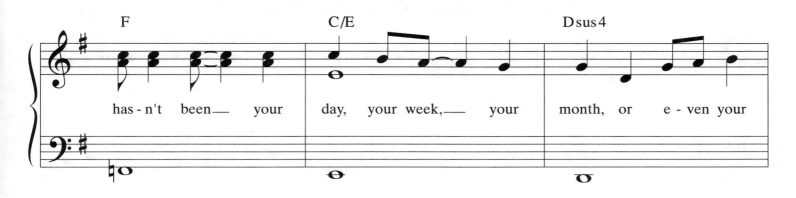

has-n't been— your | day, your week,— your | month, or e - ven your

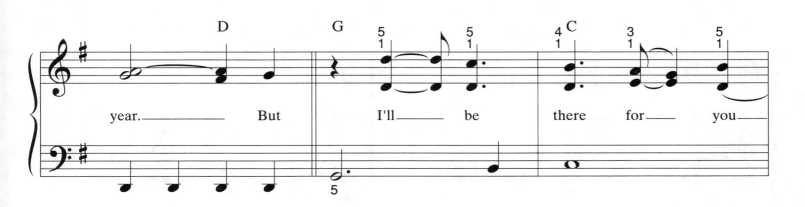

year.———— But | I'll—— be | there for— you—

— when the | rain starts—— to | fall. I'll—— be

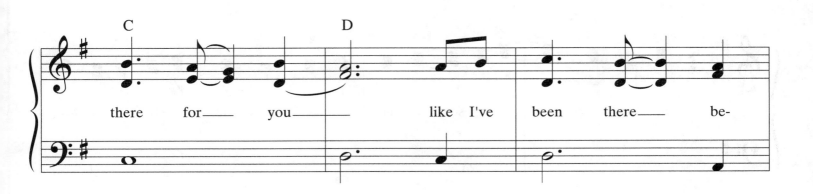

there for— you—— | like I've | been there— be-

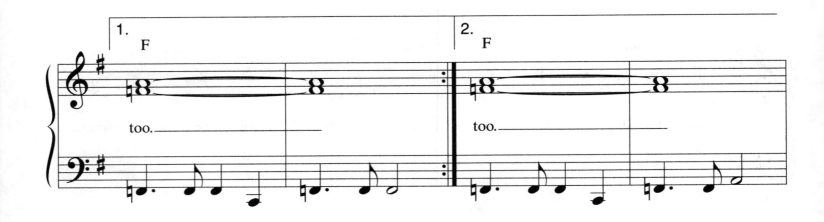

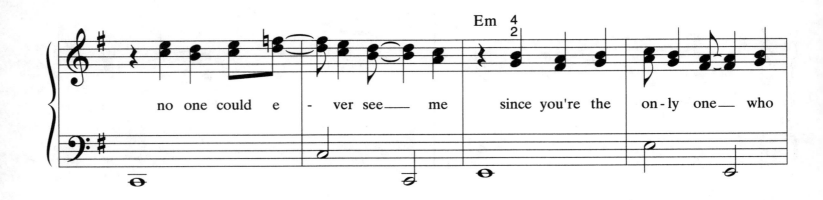

knows   what it's   like to be—— me.   Some-one—— to

face the day—— with,   make it—— through   all the rest—— with,

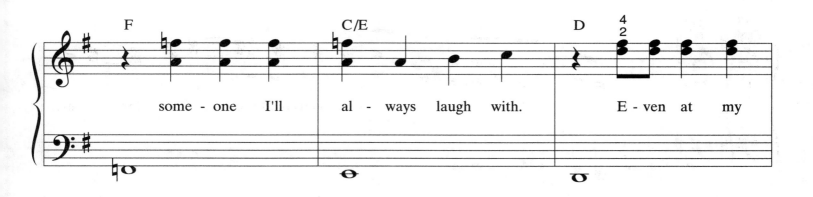

some - one I'll   al - ways laugh with.   E - ven at my

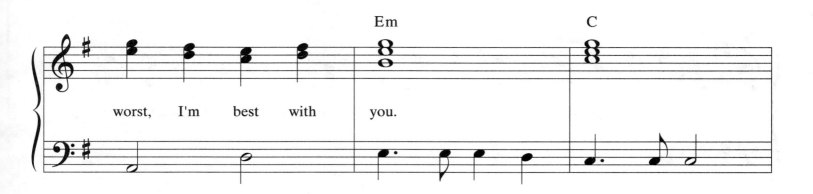

worst, I'm best with   you.

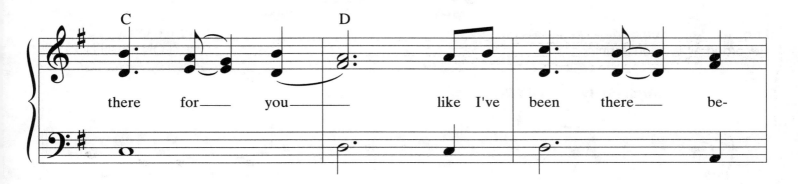

there for____ you_____ like I've been there____ be-

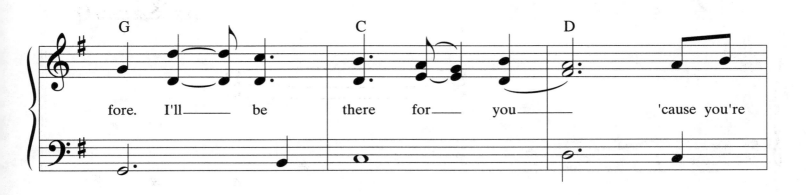

fore. I'll____ be there for____ you_____ 'cause you're

there for___ me, too._____

Verse 2:
You're still in bed at ten and work began at eight.
You've burned your breakfast, so far, everything is great.
Your mother warned you there'd be days like these,
But she didn't tell you when the world has brought you down to your knees, that
(To Chorus:)

GOOD OL' BOYS

From the Television Series *The Dukes of Hazzard*
Recorded by Waylon Jennings

Words and Music by
WAYLON JENNINGS
Arranged by Richard Bradley

1. Just the good ol'—— boys, nev-er mean-in' no

harm. Beats all you ev-er saw, been in

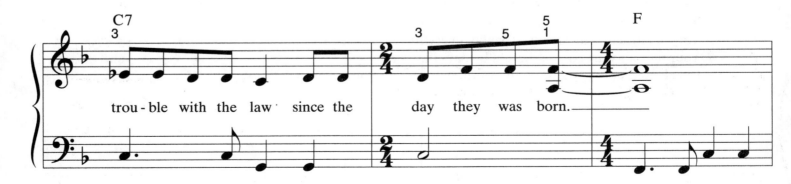

trou-ble with the law since the day they was born.

(Instrumental)

Mak - in' their

Just the good ol'—— boys,
2., 3.(Instrumental)

would-n't change_____ if they could.

Fight-in' the sys - tem like a true mod-ern day_____ Rob-in

Hood.

THE THEME FROM
"THE ANDY GRIFFITH SHOW"
("THE FISHIN' HOLE")

From the TV Series *The Andy Griffith Show*

Lyric by EVERETT SLOANE
Music by EARLE HAGEN and HERBERT SPENCER
Arranged by Richard Bradley

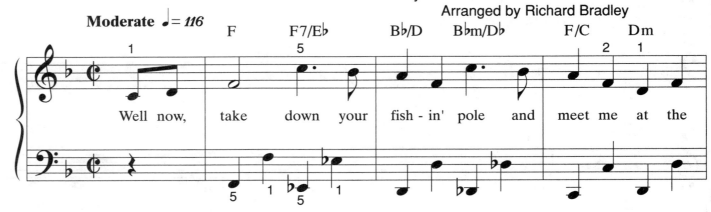

Well now, take down your fish - in' pole and meet me at the

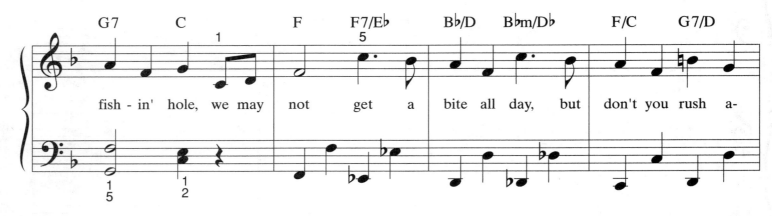

fish - in' hole, we may not get a bite all day, but don't you rush a-

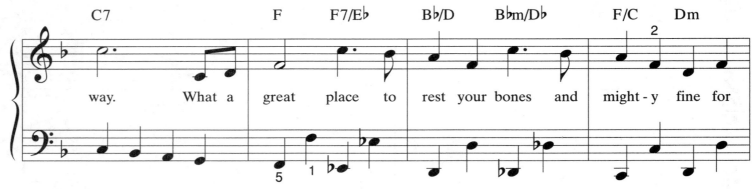

way. What a great place to rest your bones and might - y fine for

skip - pin' stones, you'll feel fresh as a lem - on - aide, a-

The Theme from "The Andy Griffith Show" - 2 - 1

THE BALLAD OF GILLIGAN'S ISLE

Theme from the TV Series *Gilligan's Island*

Words and Music by
SHERWOOD SCHWARTZ
and GEORGE WYLE
Arranged by Richard Bradley

Lovely ♩ = 82

Just sit right back and you'll hear a tale, a tale of a fate-ful

trip, that start-ed from this trop-ic port a - board this ti - ny

ship. The mate was a might-y sail-in' man, the skip-per brave and

sure, five pas-sen-gers set sail that day for a three ho-ur

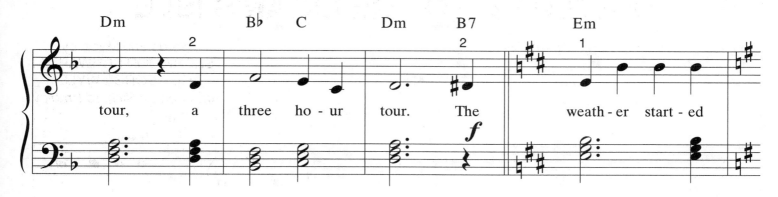

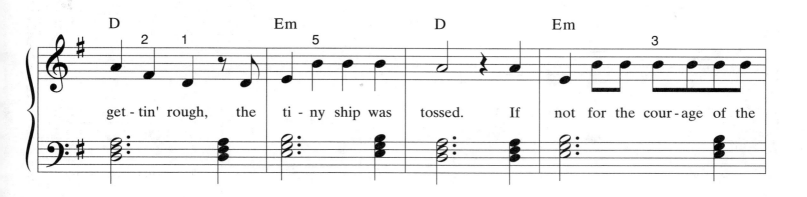

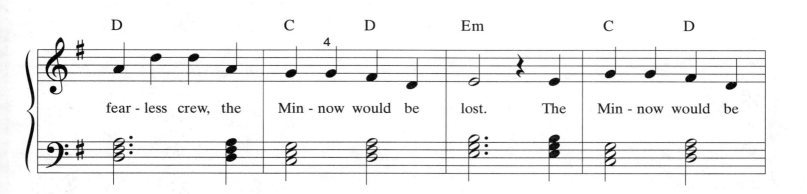

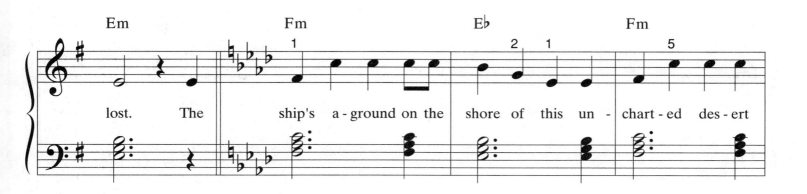

isle, with Gil - li - gan, the skip - per, too,

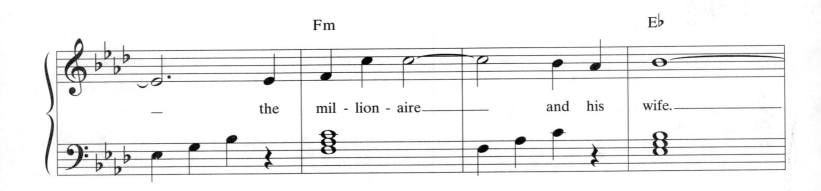

the mil - lion - aire and his wife.

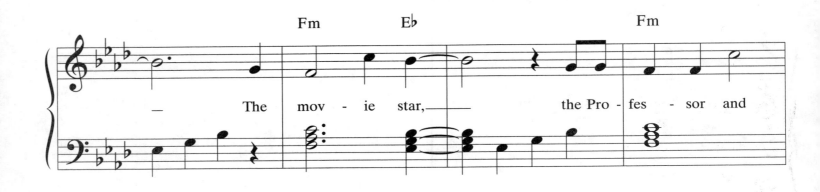

The mov - ie star, the Pro - fes - sor and

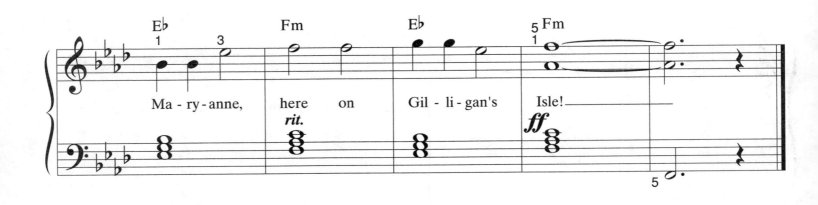

Ma - ry - anne, here on Gil - li - gan's Isle!

rit.

AMERICA, THE BEAUTIFUL

Words by KATHERINE LEE BATES
Music by SAMUEL A. WARD
Arranged by Richard Bradley

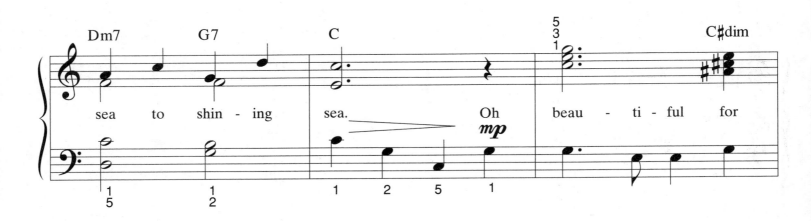

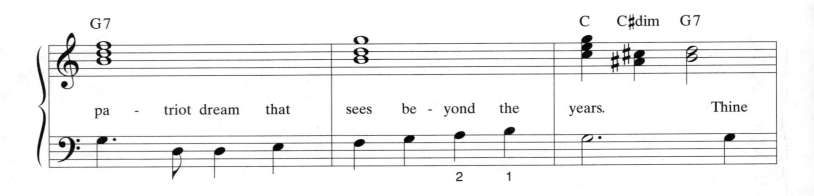

America the Beautiful - 3 - 2

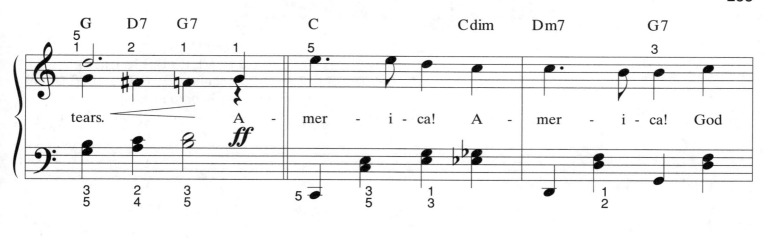

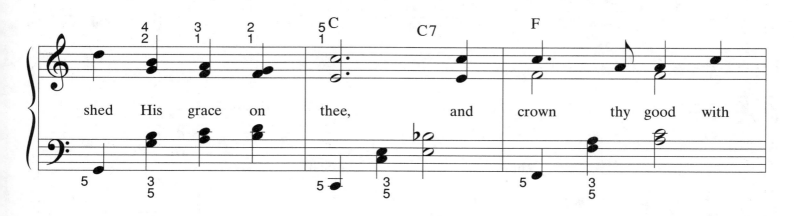

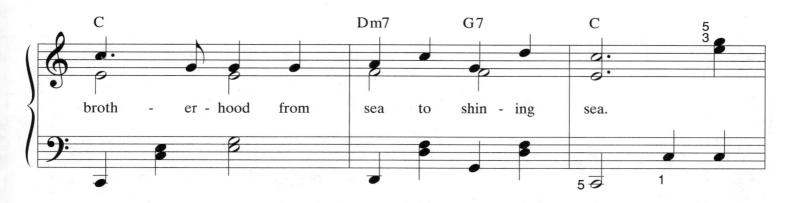

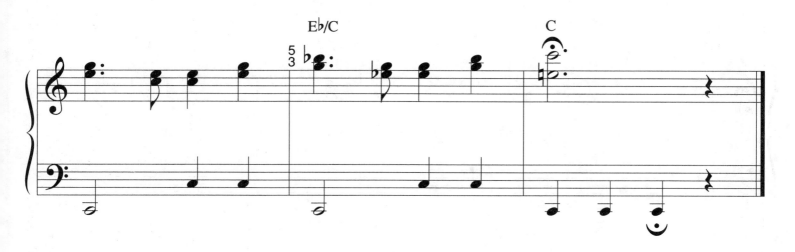

ANCHORS AWEIGH

Words and Music by
Captain ALFRED H. MILES U.S.N. (RET.),
CHARLES A. ZIMMERMAN and GEORGE D. LOTTMAN
Arranged by Richard Bradley

Through   our   last   night   on   shore,

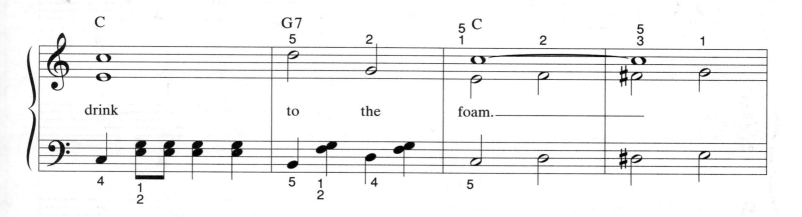

drink   to   the   foam.____

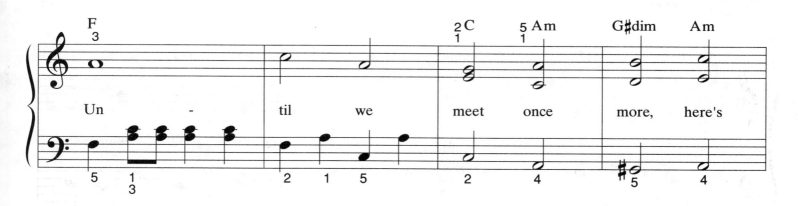

Un —   til   we   meet   once   more,   here's

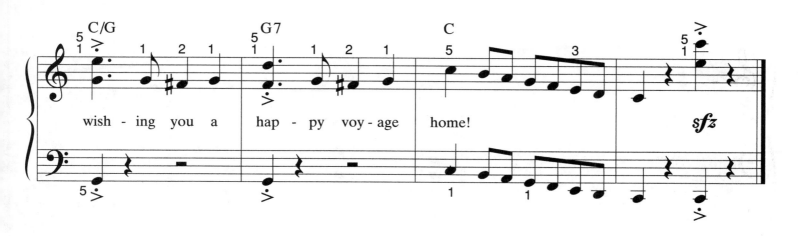

wish - ing   you   a   hap - py   voy - age   home!

sfz

THE U.S. AIR FORCE
(THE WILD BLUE YONDER)

Words and Music by
ROBERT CRAWFORD
Arranged by Richard Bradley

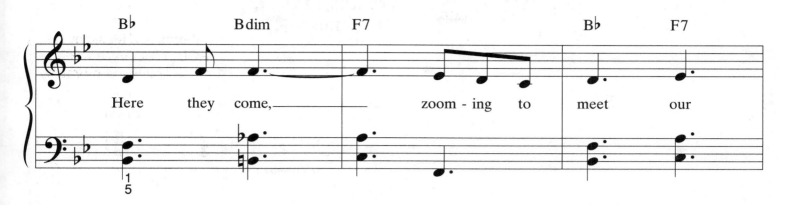

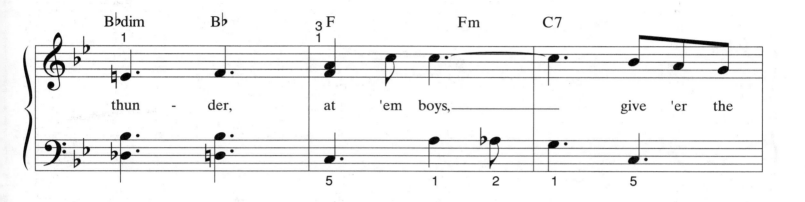

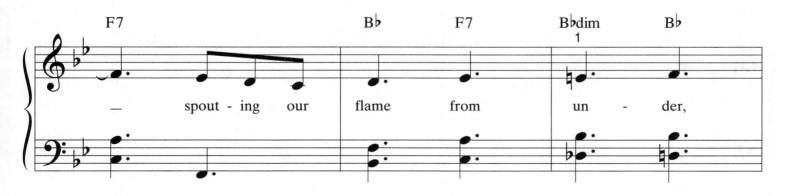

The U.S. Air Force - 3 - 2

off with one_____ ter - ri - ble roar!_____

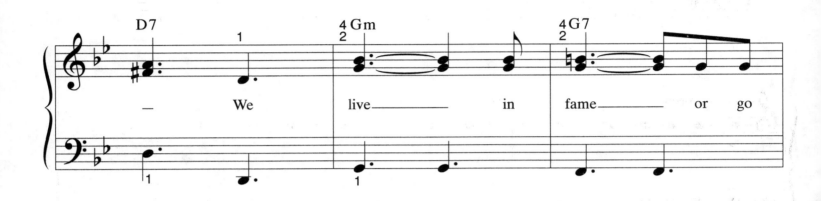

_ We live_____ in fame_____ or go

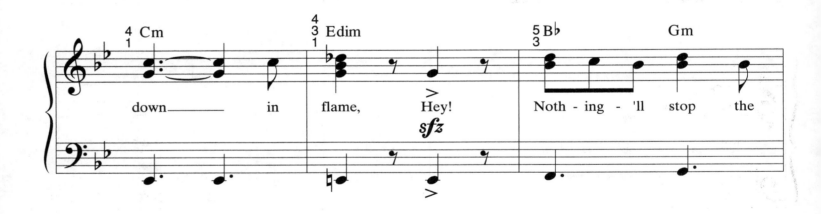

down_____ in flame, Hey! Noth - ing - 'll stop the

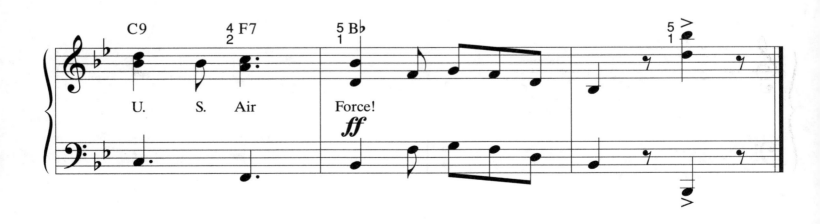

U. S. Air Force!

THE CAISSONS GO ROLLING ALONG
(U.S. FIELD ARTILLERY SONG)

By EDMUND L. GRUBER
Arranged by Richard Bradley

Bright march ♩ = 98

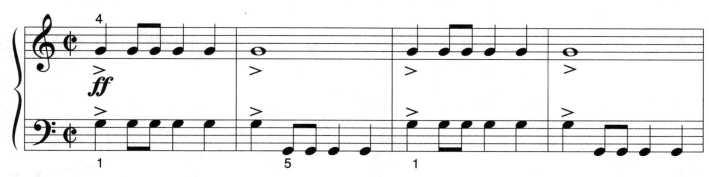

O - ver

hill,   o - ver   dale,   as   we   hit   the   dust - y   trail,   and   those

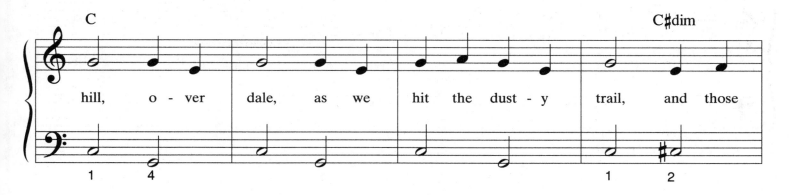

cais - sons   go   roll - ing   a - long._____   Coun - ter

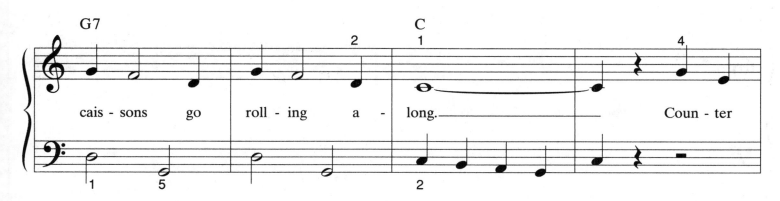

The Caissons Go Rolling Along - 3 - 1

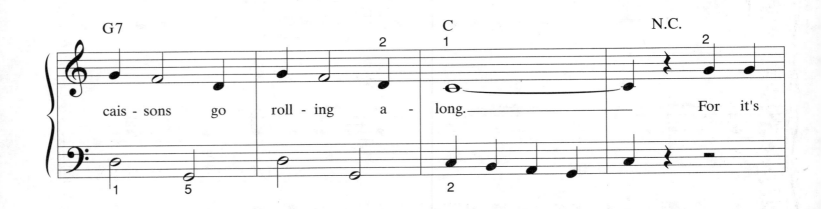

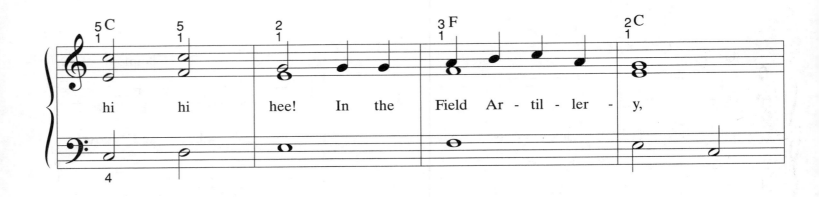

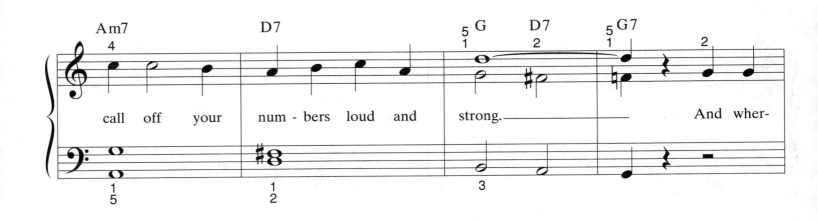

The Caissons Go Rolling Along - 3 - 2

THE MARINE'S HYMN
(FROM THE HALLS OF MONTEZUMA)

Words by L. Z. PHILLIPS
Music based on a theme by JACQUES OFFENBACH
Arranged by Richard Bradley

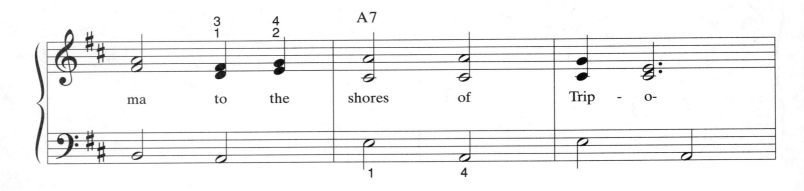

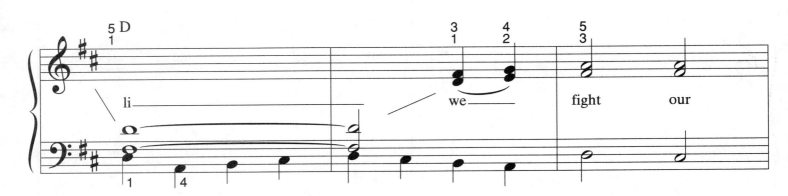

The Marines Hymn - 3 - 1

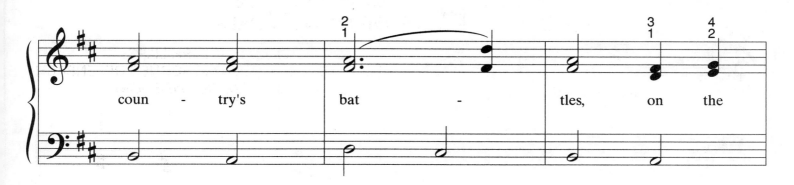

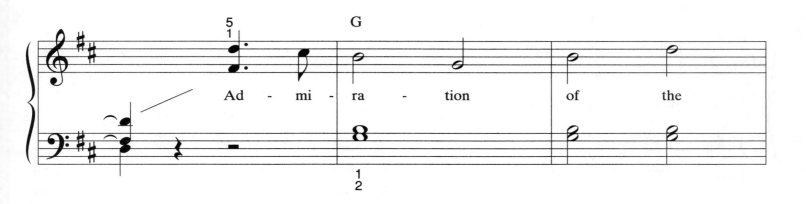

e - ver   seen,_____ and we

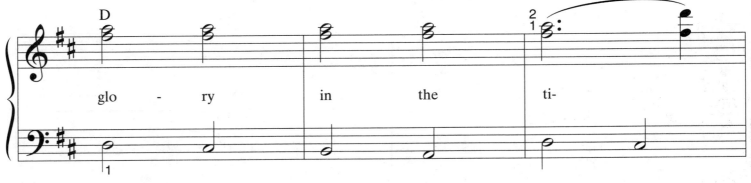

glo - ry   in   the   ti-

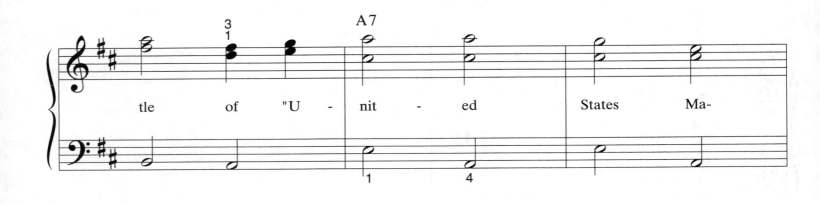

tle   of   "U - nit - ed   States   Ma-

rine."

YOU'RE A GRAND OLD FLAG

Words and Music by
GEORGE M. COHAN
Arranged by Richard Bradley

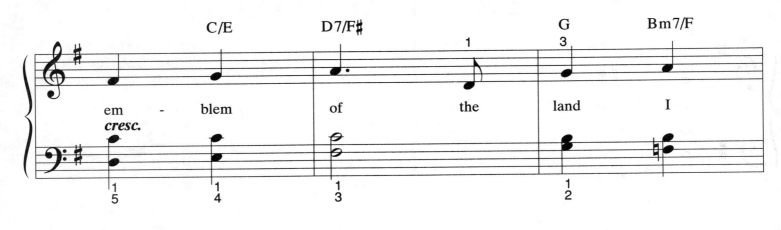

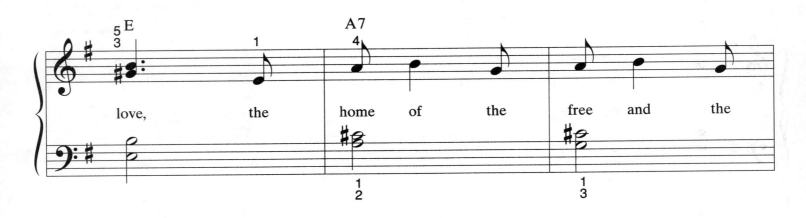

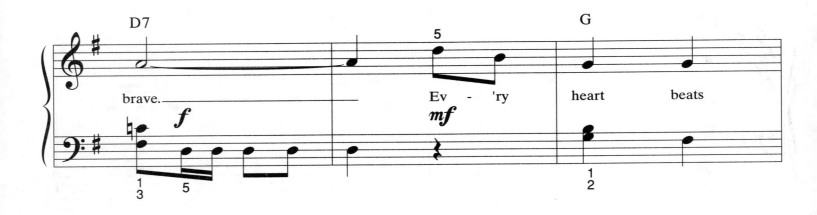

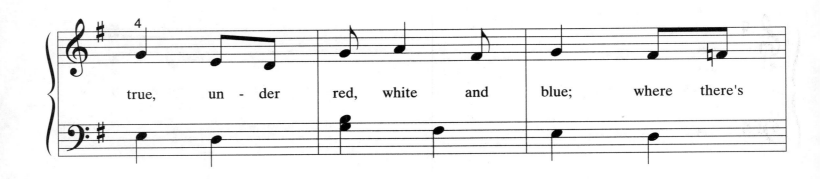

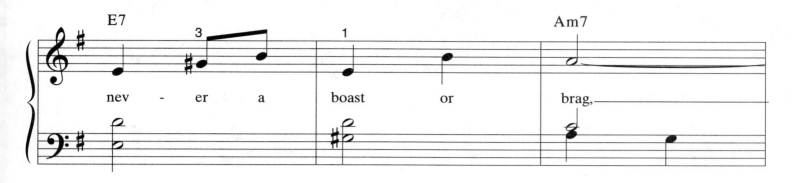

nev - er a boast or brag,

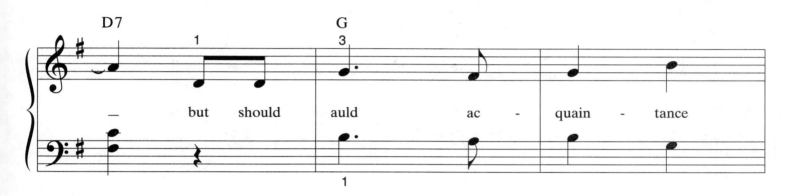

— but should auld ac - quain - tance

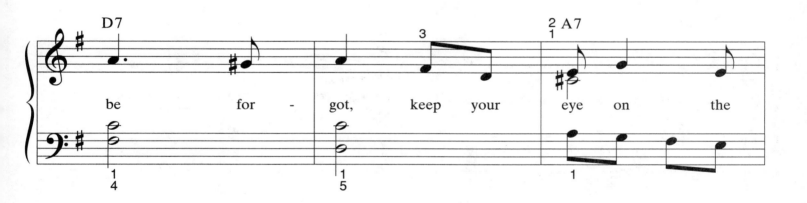

be for - got, keep your eye on the

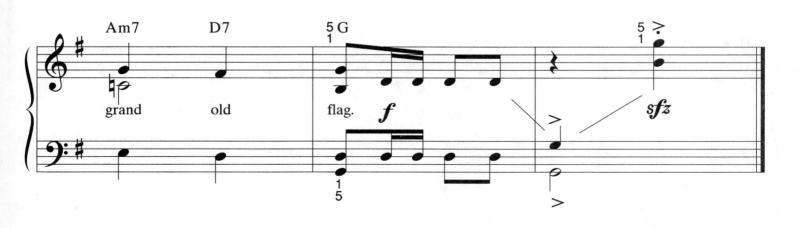

grand old flag.

THE STARS AND STRIPES FOREVER

By JOHN PHILIP SOUSA
Arranged by Richard Bradley

The Stars and Stripes Forever - 4 - 2

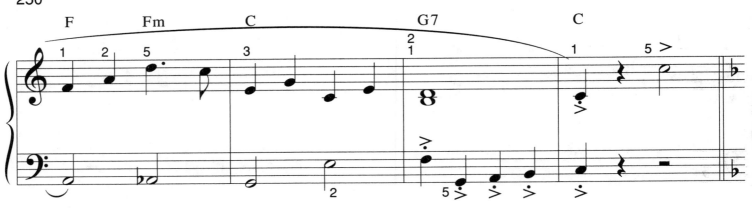

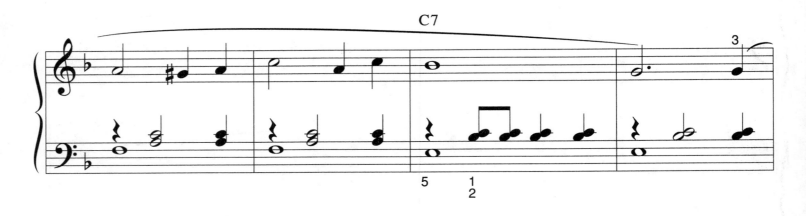

The Stars and Stripes Forever - 4 - 4

WHEN JOHNNY COMES MARCHING HOME

TRADITIONAL
Arranged by Richard Bradley

When Johnny comes march - ing home a - gain, Hur-
rah!____ Hur - rah!____ We'll give him a heart - y
wel - come then, Hur - rah!_____ Hur - rah!_____ The____

When Johnny Comes Marching Home - 3 - 1

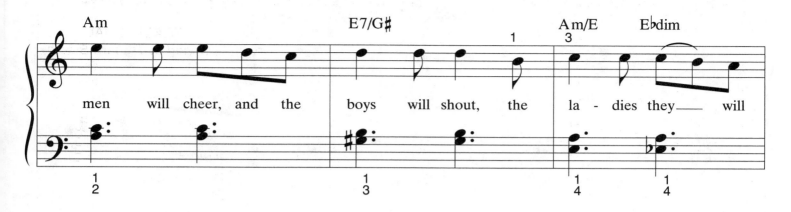

THE BATTLE HYMN OF THE REPUBLIC

Words by JULIA WARD HOWE
Music by WILLIAM STEFFE
Arranged by Richard Bradley

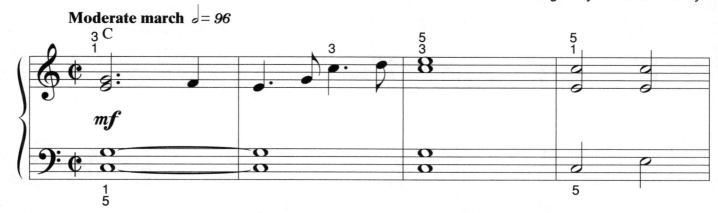

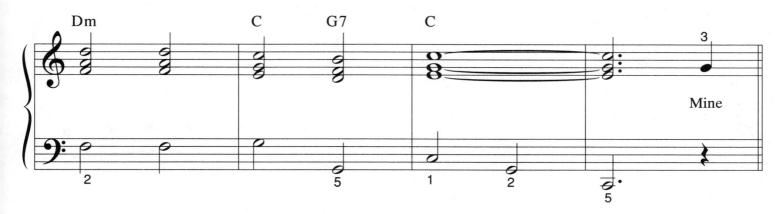

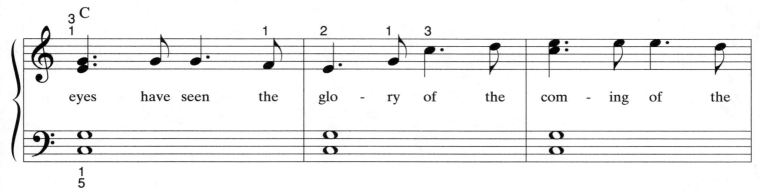

The Battle Hymn of the Republic - 3 - 1

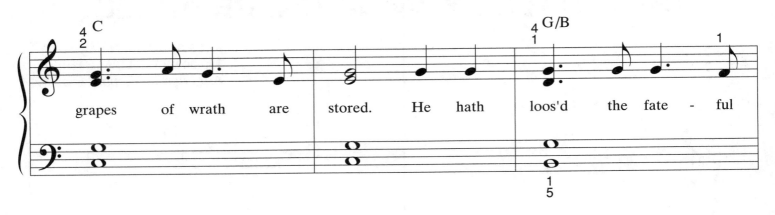

grapes of wrath are stored. He hath loos'd the fate - ful

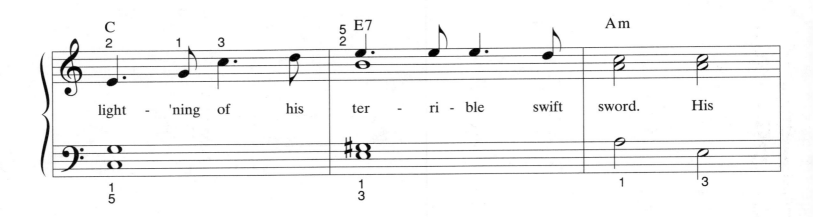

light - 'ning of his ter - ri - ble swift sword. His

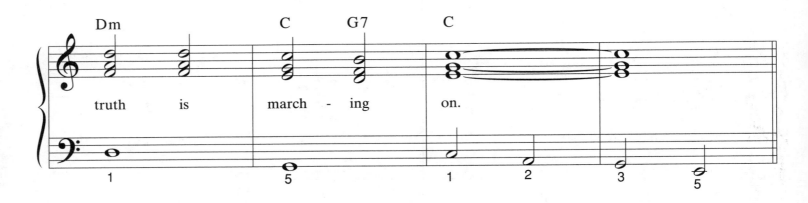

truth is march - ing on.

Glo - ry, Glo - ry, Hal - le - lu - jah!

The Battle Hymn of the Republic - 3 - 2

Additional Lyrics:

2. I have seen Him in the watch-fires of a hundred circling camps.
   They have builded Him an alter in the evening dews and damps.
   I have read his righteous sentence by the dim and flaring lamps.
   His day is marching on.
   (Chorus:)

3. I have read a fiery gospel writ in burnished rows of steel,
   "As ye deal with my contempters, so with you my grace shall deal."
   Let the hero born of woman crush the serpent with his heel,
   Since God is marching on.
   (Chorus:)

4. He has sounded forth the trumpet that shall never call retreat.
   He is sifting out the hearts of men before His judgement seat.
   O be swift, my soul, to answer Him, be jubilant my feet,
   Our God is marching on.
   (Chorus:)

The Battle Hymn of the Republic - 3 - 3

YANKEE DOODLE

TRADITIONAL
Arranged by Richard Bradley

Fath'r and I went down to camp a - long with Cap - tain

Good - 'in, and there we saw the men and boys as

thick as has - ty pud - din'.

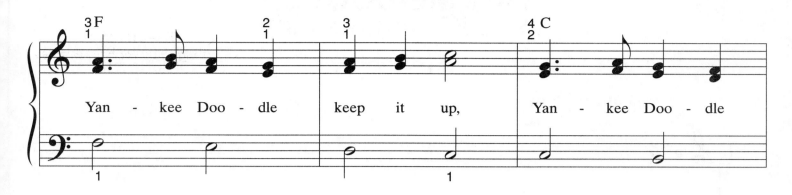

Yan - kee Doo - dle keep it up, Yan - kee Doo - dle

Dan - dy, mind the mu - sic and the step, and

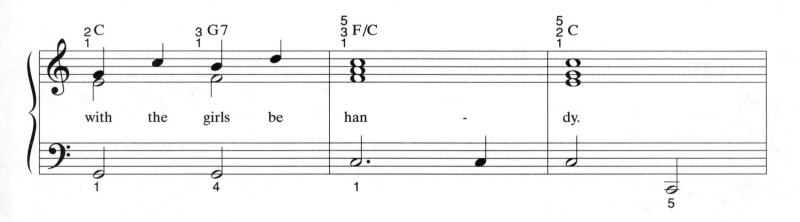

with the girls be han - dy.

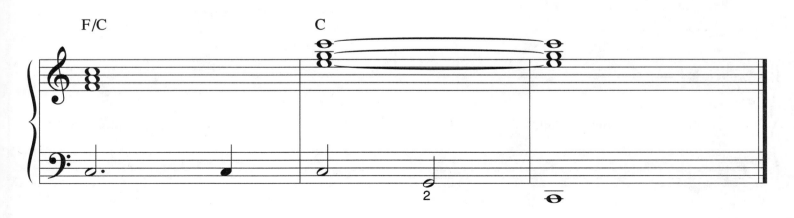

AMERICA
(MY COUNTRY 'TIS OF THEE)

Words by SAMUEL F. SMITH
TRADITIONAL MELODY
Arranged by Richard Bradley

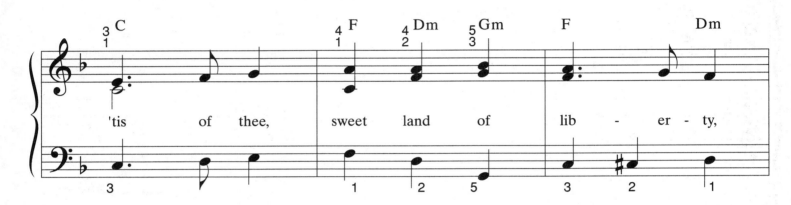

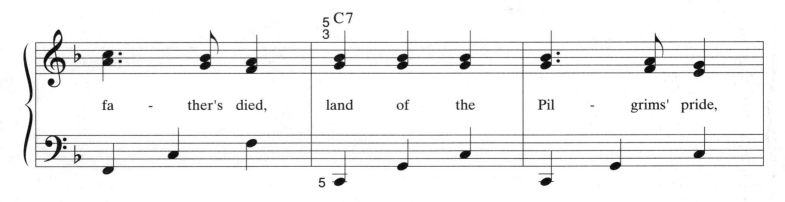

America - 2 - 1

THE STAR-SPANGLED BANNER

Words by FRANCIS SCOTT KEY
Music by JOHN STAFFORD SMITH
Arranged by Richard Bradley

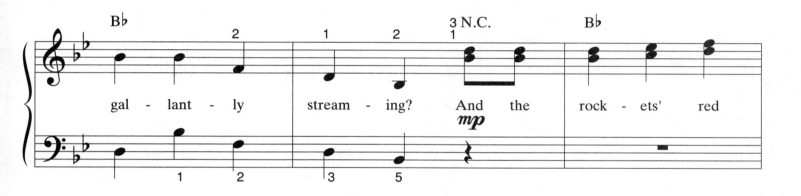

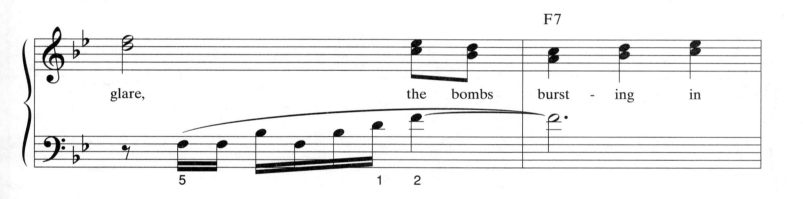

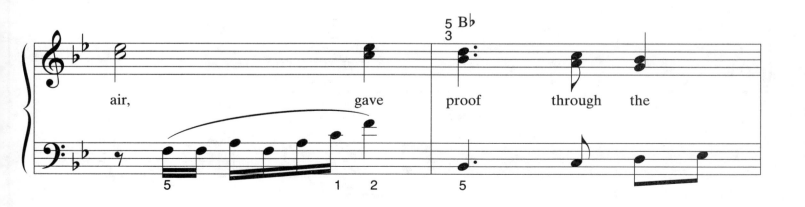

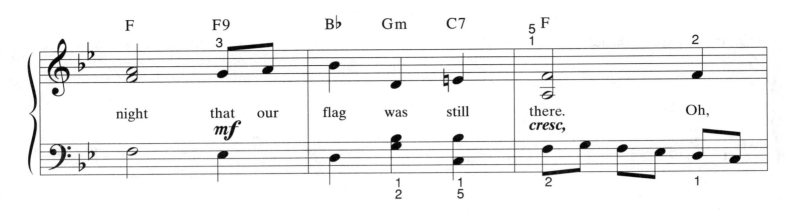

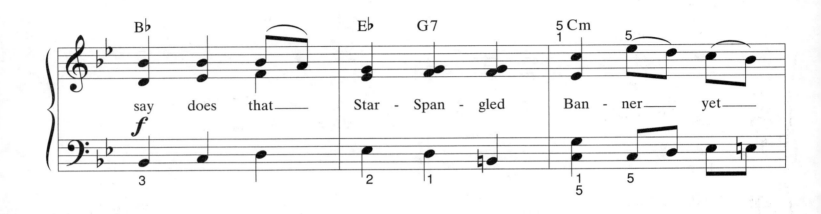

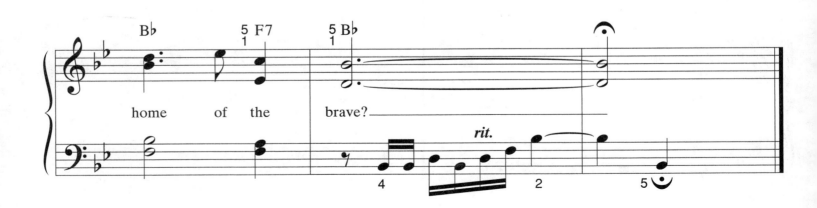

HEART

From the Broadway Musical *Damn Yankees*

Words and Music by
RICHARD ADLER and JERRY ROSS
Arranged by Richard Bradley

noth-in's half as bad as it may ap-pear,____ wait-'ll next year____ and

hope. When your luck is bat-tin' ze-ro,____

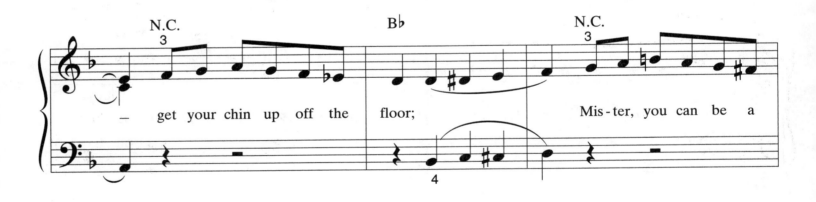

___ get your chin up off the floor; Mis-ter, you can be a

he-ro, you can o-pen an-y door, there's noth-in' to it, but to

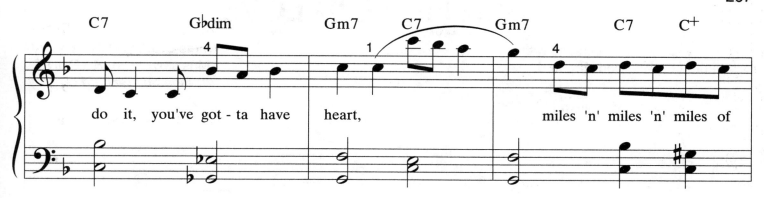

do it, you've got - ta have heart, miles 'n' miles 'n' miles of

heart. Oh, it's fine to be a gen - ius of course,——— but

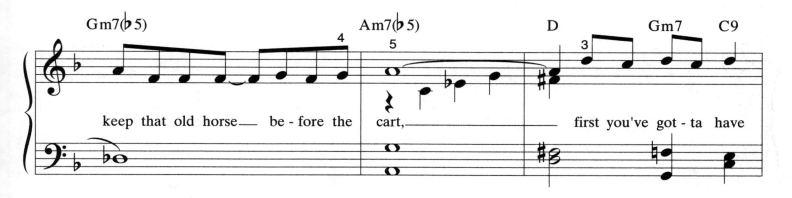

keep that old horse— be - fore the cart,————————— first you've got - ta have

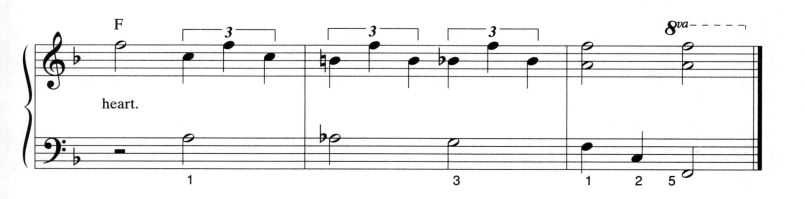

heart.

WHEN I FALL IN LOVE

Nat "King" Cole had the first hit with
this frequently recorded standard.

Words by EDWARD HEYMAN
Music by VICTOR YOUNG
Arranged by Richard Bradley

rest - less world like this is,————— love is

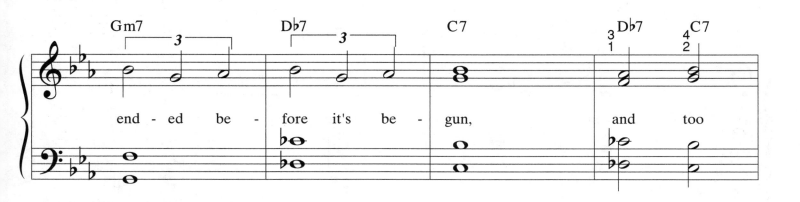

end - ed be - fore it's be - gun, and too

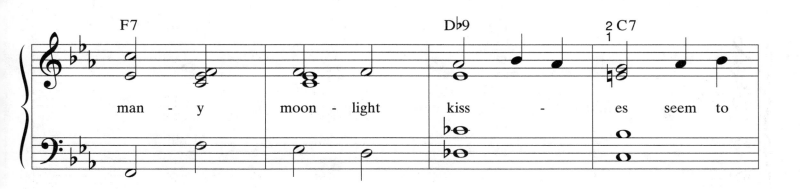

man - y moon - light kiss - es seem to

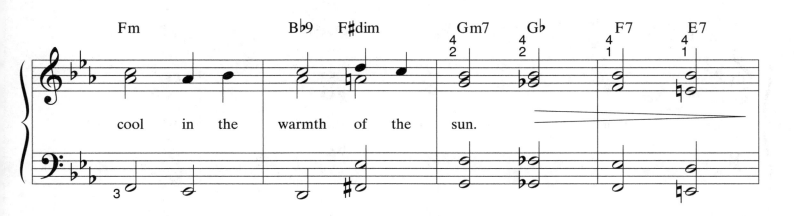

cool in the warmth of the sun.

When I Fall in Love - 4 - 2

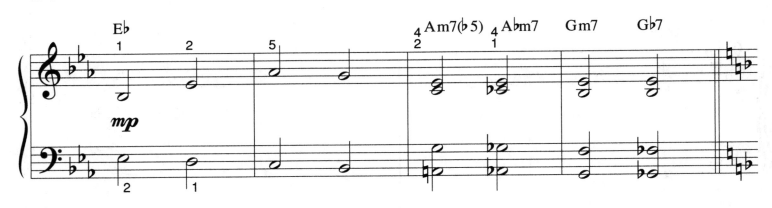

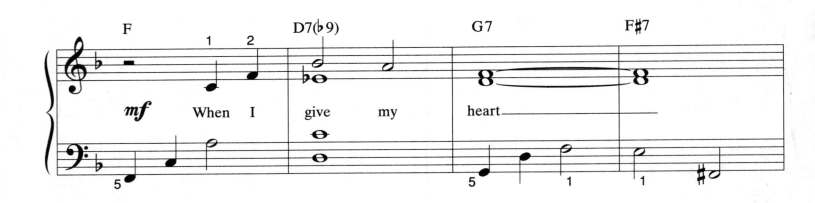

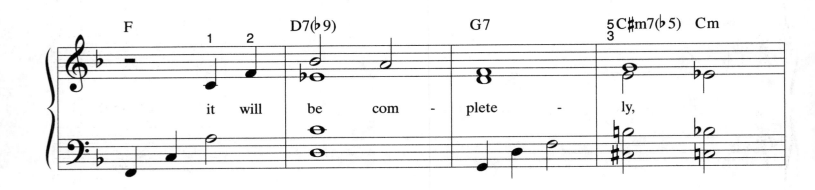

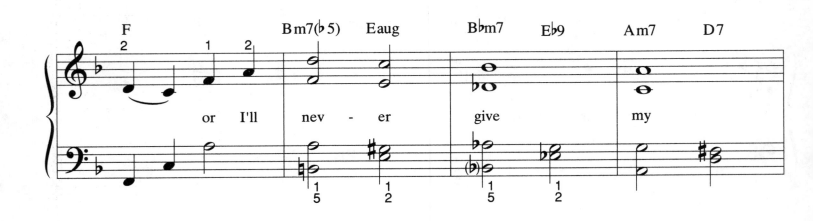

MY FUNNY VALENTINE

This standard from the Broadway Musical *Babes in Arms* was also featured in the film *Pal Joey*.

Words by LORENZ HART
Music by RICHARD RODGERS
Arranged by Richard Bradley

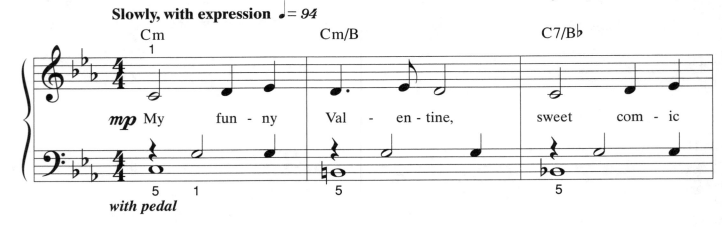

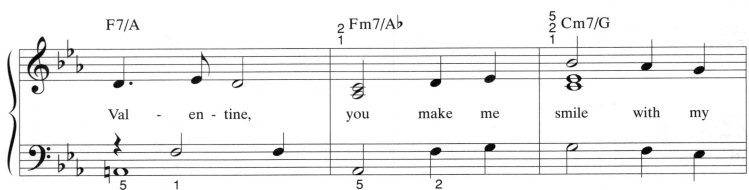

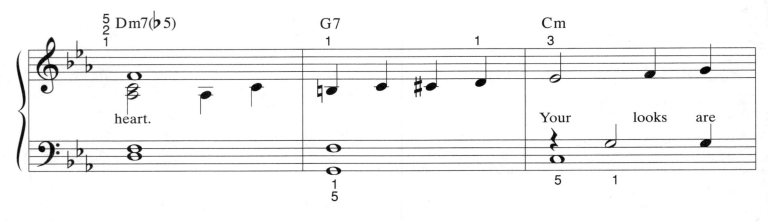

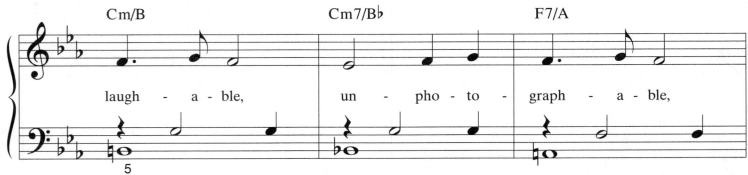

My Funny Valentine - 3 - 1

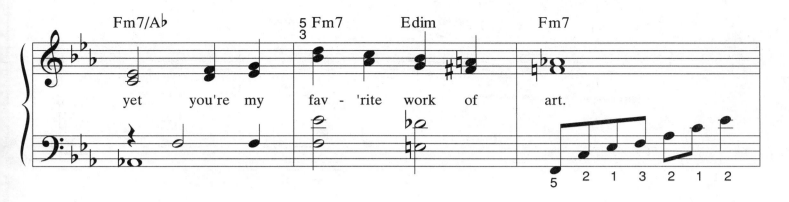

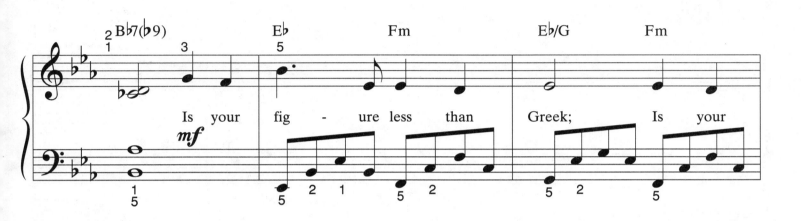

274

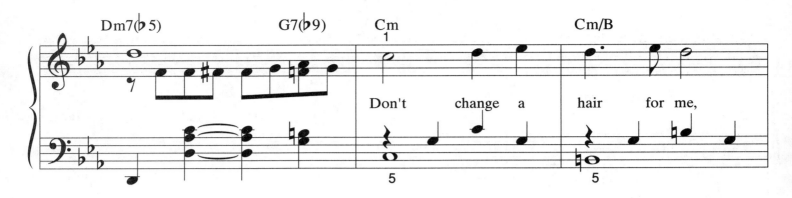

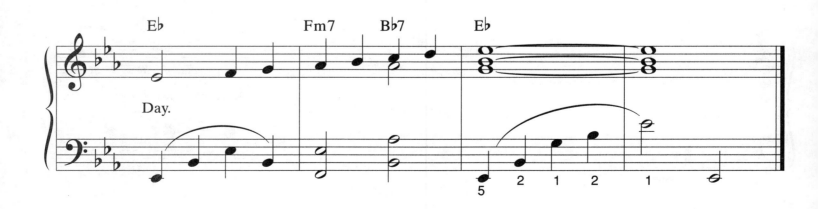

AT LAST

Originally recorded by Glenn Miller & his Orchestra, *At Last* is sung by Etta James on the soundtrack of the motion picture *Living Out Loud*.

Lyric by MACK GORDON
Music by HARRY WARREN
Arranged by Richard Bradley

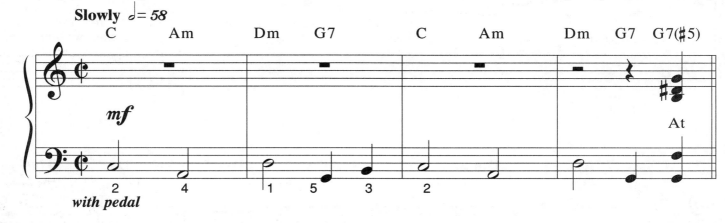

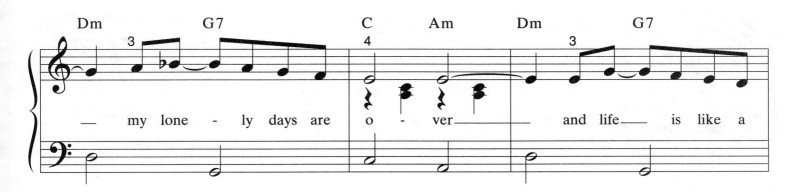

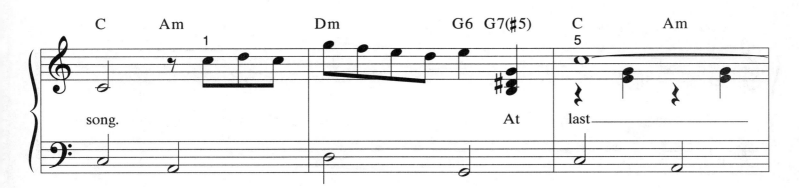

At Last - 3 - 1

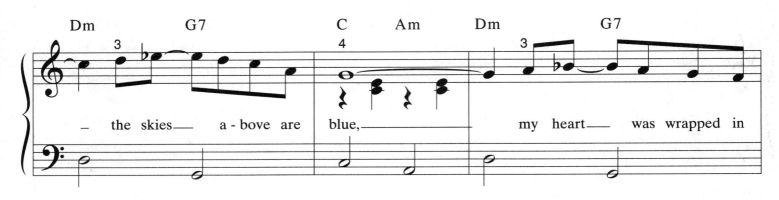

the skies — a-bove are blue, — my heart — was wrapped in

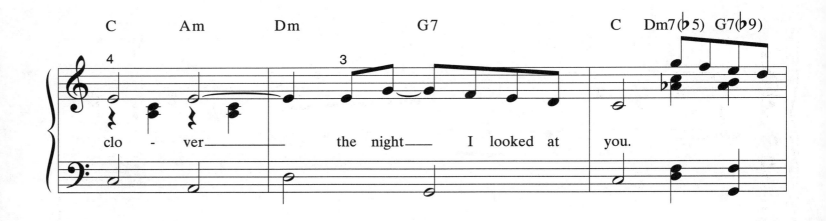

clo - ver — the night — I looked at you.

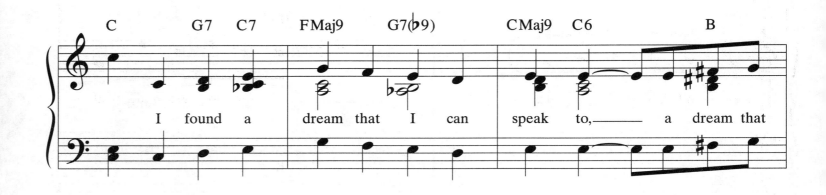

I found a dream that I can speak to, — a dream that

I can call my own, — I found a thrill to press my

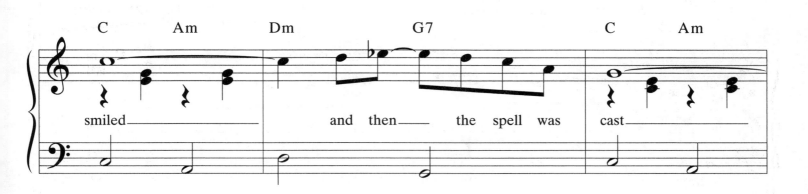

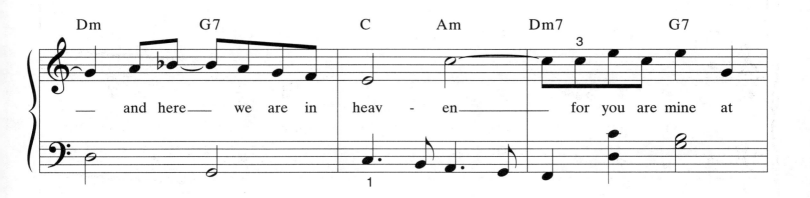

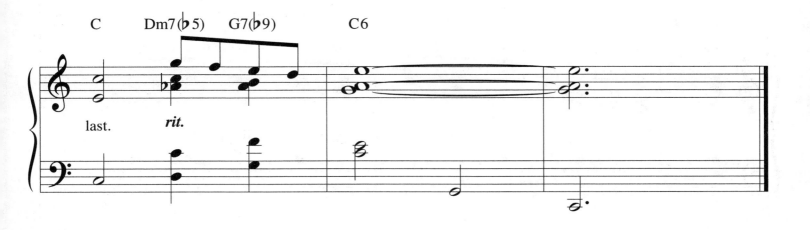

SOMEONE TO WATCH OVER ME

From the Broadway Musical *Oh, Kay!*

Music and Lyrics by
GEORGE GERSHWIN and IRA GERSHWIN
Arranged by Richard Bradley

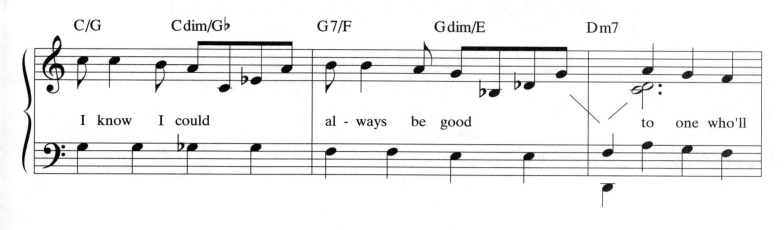

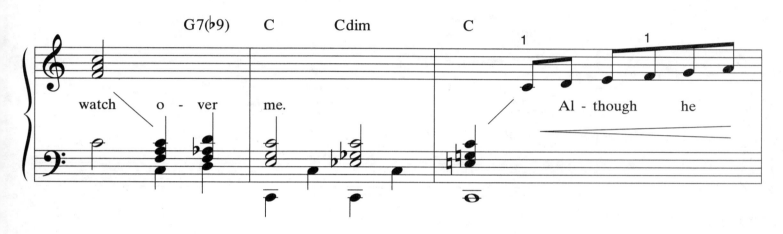

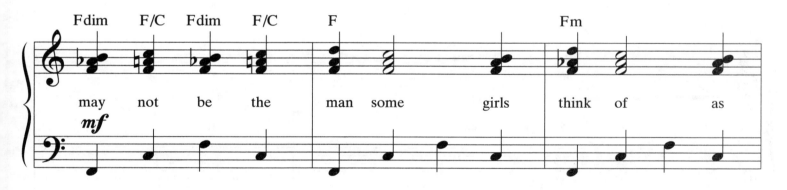

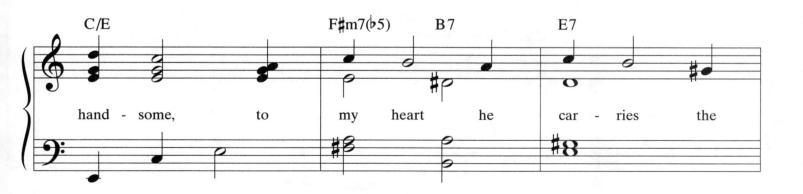

280

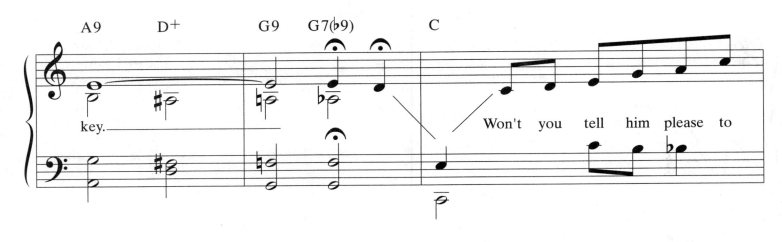

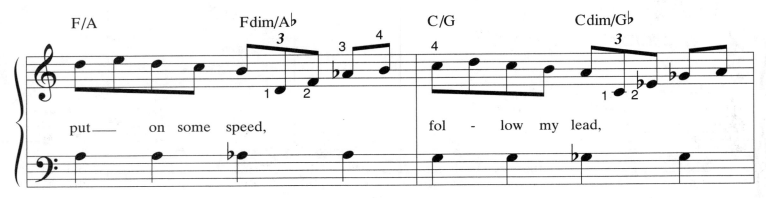

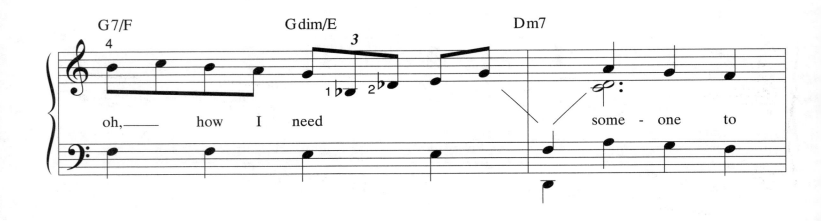

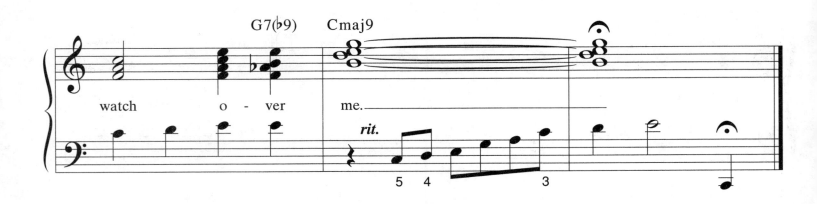

Someone To Watch Over Me - 3 - 3

EBB TIDE

Frank Chacksfield & his Orchestra and Stanley Black
& his Orchestra had popular recordings of this standard.

Lyric by CARL SIGMAN
Music by ROBERT MAXWELL
Arranged by Richard Bradley

wide? At last we're face to face, and as we

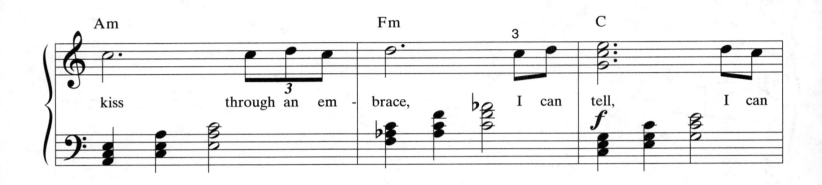

kiss through an em - brace, I can tell, I can

feel, you are love, you are real, real - ly

mine in the rain, in the

IT'S DE-LOVELY

Robbie Williams sings this standard in the
Cole Porter biographical film *De-Lovely*.

Words and Music by
COLE PORTER
Arranged by Richard Bradley

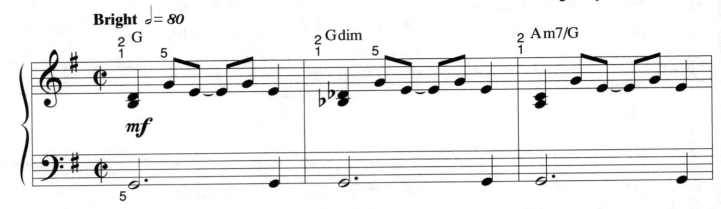

The night is young, the skies are clear, so

if you want to go walk-ing, dear, it's de-light-ful, it's de-

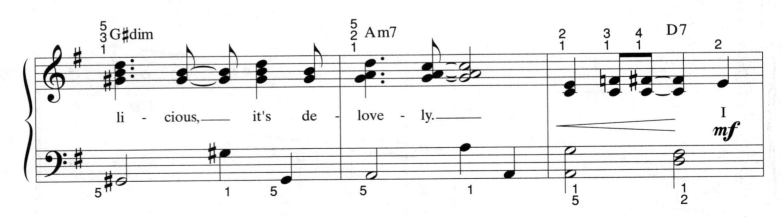

li - cious, it's de - love - ly.

It's De-Lovely - 4 - 1

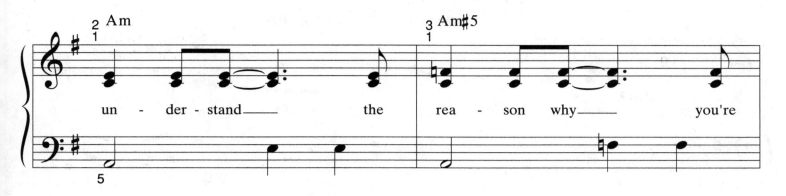

un - der - stand____ the rea - son why____ you're

sen - ti - men - tal, 'cause so am I.____ It's de-

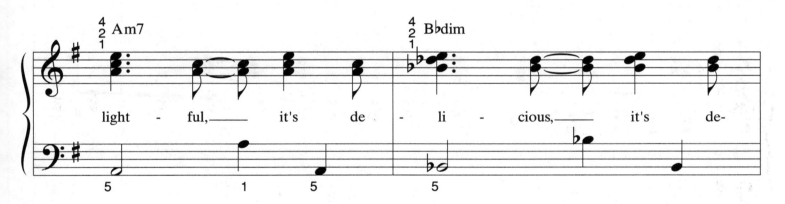

light - ful,____ it's de - li - cious,____ it's de-

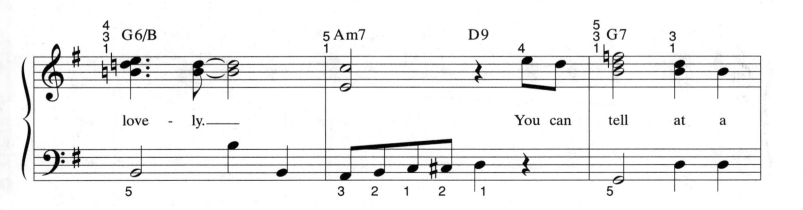

love - ly.____ You can tell at a

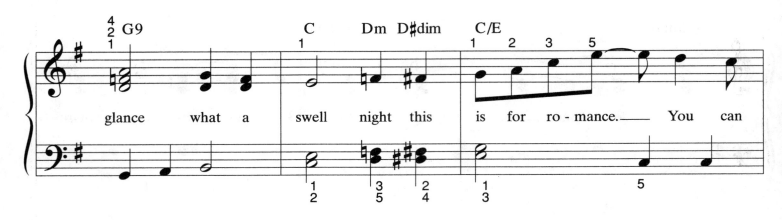

glance   what a   swell   night   this   is   for   ro - mance.   You   can

hear   dear   Moth - er   Na - ture   mur - mur - ing   low,

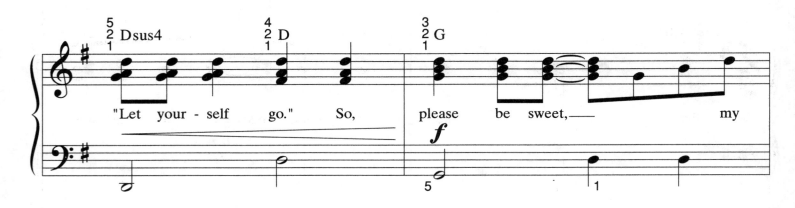

"Let   your - self   go."   So,   please   be   sweet,   my

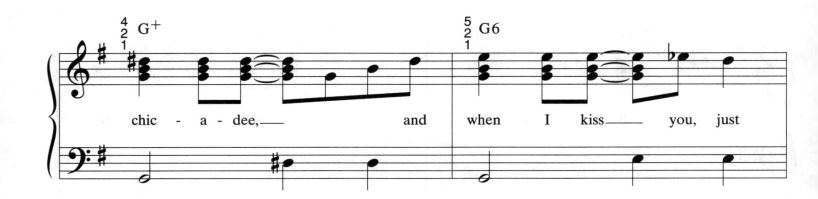

chic - a - dee,   and   when   I   kiss   you,   just

WHAT A WONDERFUL WORLD

Louis Armstrong's recording of this
standard is still frequently heard today.

Words and Music by
GEORGE DAVID WEISS and BOB THIELE
Arranged by Richard Bradley

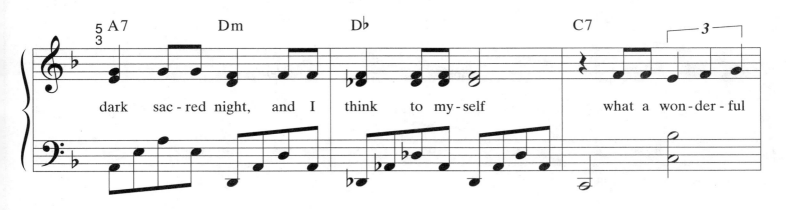

dark   sac-red night,   and I   think   to my-self   what a won-der-ful

world.   The_____   col-ors of the rain-bow, so

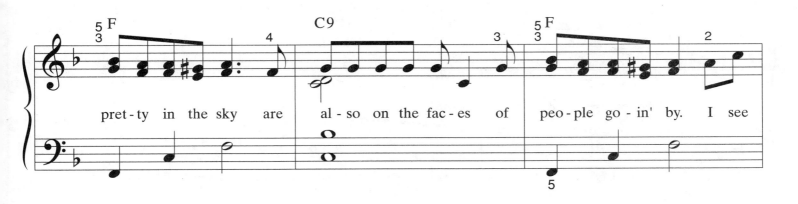

pret-ty in the sky   are   al-so on the fac-es   of   peo-ple go-in' by.   I see

friends shak-in' hands, say-in',   "How do you do!"   they're real-ly say-in'

BLUE MOON

Elvis Presley, Rosemary Clooney and Mel Tormé are just
three of the artists who have recorded this great standard.

Lyrics by LORENZ HART
Music by RICHARD RODGERS
Arranged by Richard Bradley

you knew just what I was there_____ for._____ You heard me say-ing a pray'r—

— for_____ some-one I could real-ly care for.

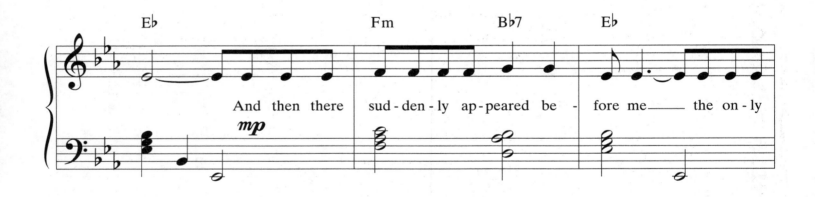

And then there sud-den-ly ap-peared be - fore me_____ the on-ly

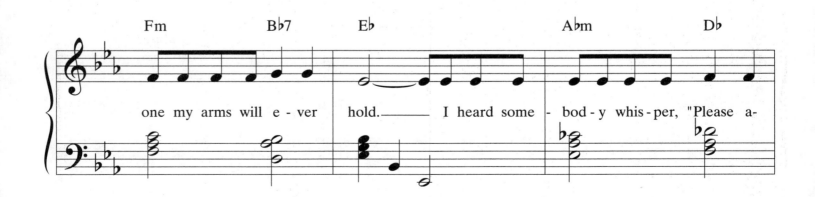

one my arms will e - ver hold._____ I heard some-bod-y whis-per, "Please a-

293

THE SECOND TIME AROUND

Bing Crosby had the first hit on this standard.
Jack Jones had a hit the second time around.

Words by SAMMY CAHN
Music by JAMES VAN HEUSEN
Arranged by Richard Bradley

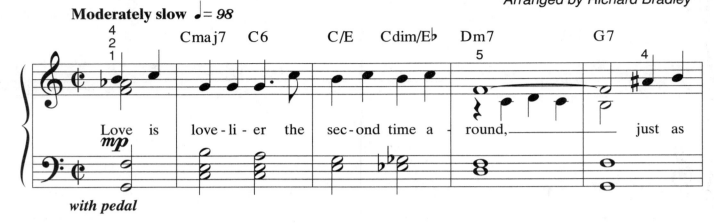

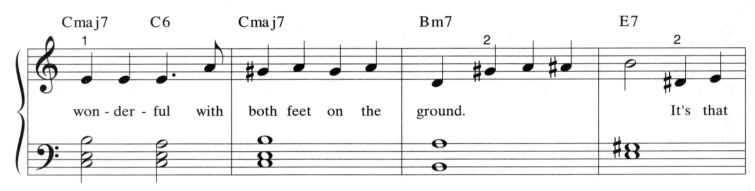

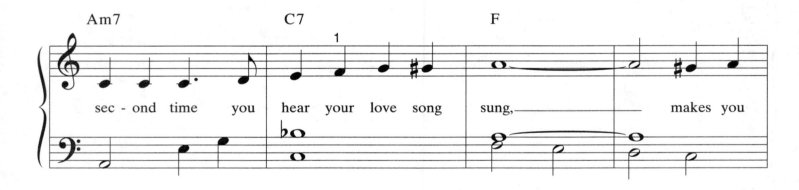

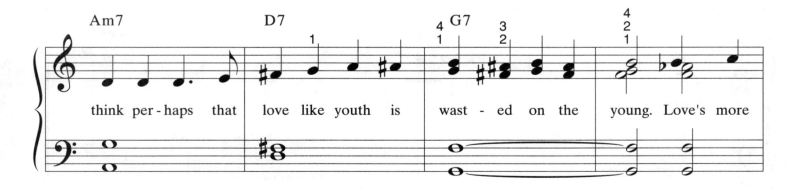

EMBRACEABLE YOU

From the Broadway Musical *Girl Crazy.*

Music and Lyrics by
GEORGE GERSHWIN and IRA GERSHWIN
Arranged by Richard Bradley

Em - brace me, my sweet em-
I love all the man - y

brace - a - ble you!
charms a - bout you:

Em - brace me, you ir - re-
a - bove all I want my

place - a - ble you!

Just one look at you, my heart grew

tip - sy in me;

You and you a-

Embraceable You - 2 - 1

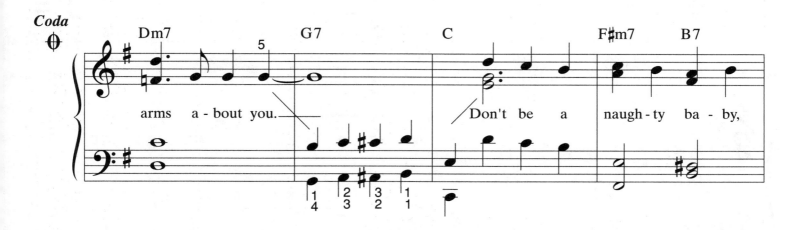

WHERE OR WHEN

From the Broadway Musical *Babes in Arms.*

Words by LORENZ HART
Music by RICHARD RODGERS
Arranged by Richard Bradley

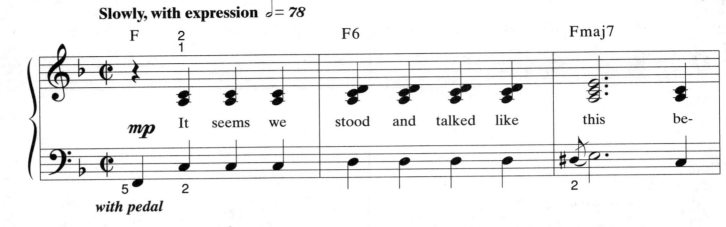

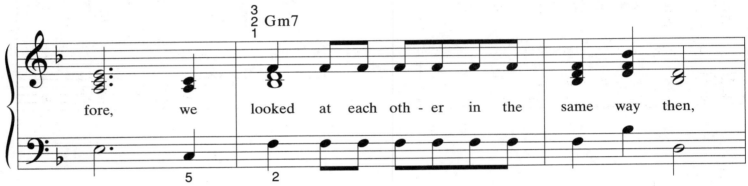

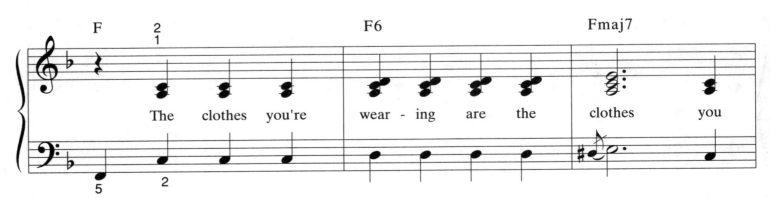

Where or When - 3 - 1

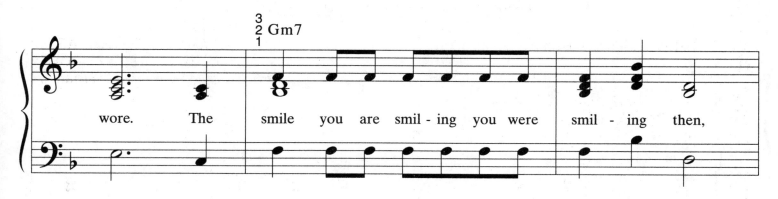

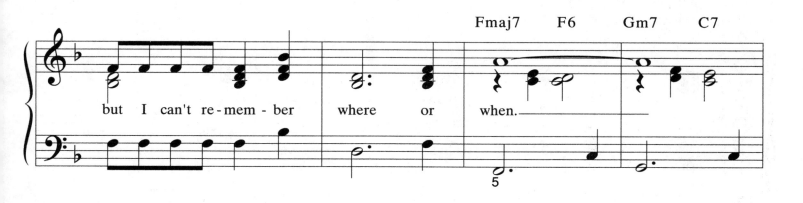

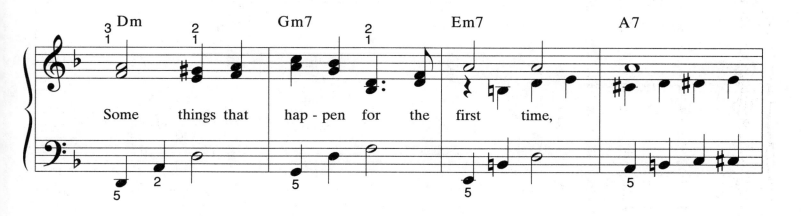

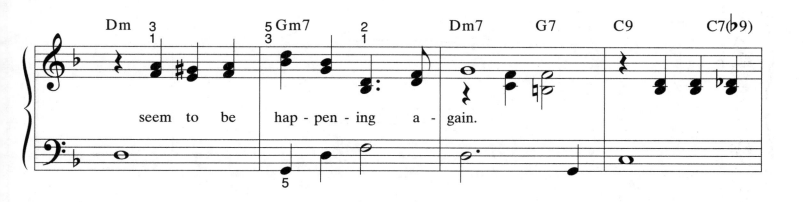

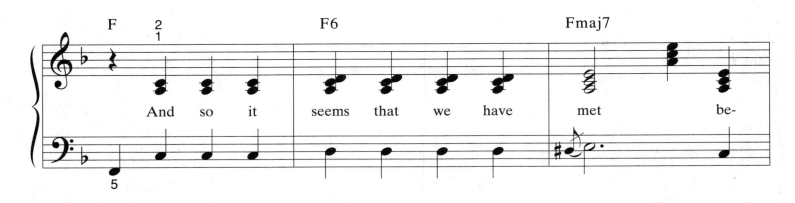

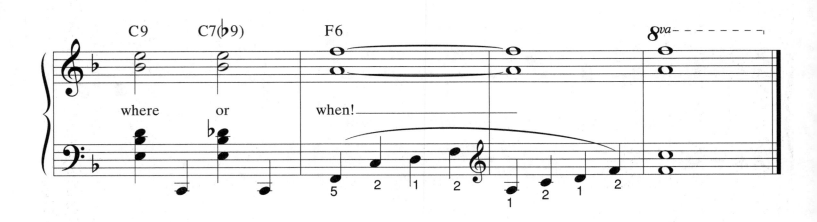

MISTY

The Erroll Garner Trio were the first to record this standard.
Johnny Mathis had the pop hit.

Lyric by JOHNNY BURKE
Music by ERROLL GARNER
Arranged by Richard Bradley

Misty - 3 - 1

Verse 3:
On my own, would I wander through this wonderland alone,
Never knowing my right foot from my left,
My hat from my glove, I'm too misty and too much in love.

Misty - 3 - 3